WALKING
THE
POINT

MALE INITIATION AND
THE VIETNAM EXPERIENCE

by

Daryl S. Paulson, Ph.D.

Foreword by Stanley Krippner, Ph.D.

Preface by Michael Washburn, Ph.D.

dp
DISTINCTIVE PUBLISHING

Walking The Point: Male Initiation and the Vietnam Experience
By Daryl S. Paulson
Copyright 1994 by Daryl S. Paulson

Published by Distinctive Publishing Corp.
P.O. Box 17868
Plantation, Florida 33318-7868
Printed in the United States of America

ISBN: 0-942963-49-0
Library of Congress No.: 94-8249
Price: $8.95

Library of Congress Cataloging-in-Publication Data

Paulson, Daryl S., 1947-
        Walking the point: male initiation and the Vietnam
experience / by Daryl S. Paulson: Foreword by Stanley Krippner.
                p. cm.
        ISBN 0-942963-49-0 : $8.95
        1. Vietnamese Conflict, 1961-1975—Veterans—Mental
health. 2. Initiation rites—Psychological aspects. 3. Men—
Psychology. 4. Vietnamese Conflict, 1961-1975—Psychological
aspects.
I. Title.
RC451.4.V48P38 1994
616.85'121—dc20   94-8249

        CIP

CONTENTS

FOREWORD

From a psychological perspective, "myths" and personal mythology are not legends or falsehoods, they are rather the models by which humans code and organize their perceptions, feelings, thoughts, and actions which provide meaning. Meaning provides identity ("Who am I?"), direction ("Where am I going?"), and purpose ("How will I get there?"). Myths help people to explain their past, cope with the present, and plan their future activities. Rituals are the way people act out or perform their myths. Often, rituals are stylized, step-by-step performances, executed by mandated persons in specific places and at definite times. But rituals can also appear to be spontaneous; people can implement mythic themes unconsciously. In either event, rituals help to promote social solidarity, provide for life transitions, and reinforce values, belief systems, and rules of conduct. (Although used interchangeably with "rite" and "ceremony" by some writers, it may be useful to describe "rites" as "mini-rituals" of passage from one stage of life to another, e.g., puberty rites and funeral rites, and "ceremony" as elaborate, "maxi-rituals" that often comprise a series of rituals, e.g., coronation ceremonies and four-day Sun Dance ceremonies.)

In *Walking the Point*, Dr. Daryl Paulson makes the case that countless Vietnam combat veterans embarked on an initiatory experience—and that many of them never completed it. Western industrialized, technological societies are marked by a dearth of formal rituals and a tattered mythic legacy. As a result, combat veterans of unsuccessful and unpopular wars have had to search for sustaining myths and enact the ensuing rituals alone, without the community support that characterizes similar endeavors in native cultures. Dr. Paulson has found three recurring themes in his interviews with Vietnam veterans: a call to adventure, an initiation, and a return.

But many veterans did not work their way through the last phase of this ritual. Some mythic journeyers complete their initiation by finding a positive meaning in their experience, a private meaning that they rarely disclose. Other journeyers return to their communities with a treasured resource that they reveal and share. If neither alternative is taken, it is difficult if not impossible for the journeyer to move on to other ventures, other quests, and other life tasks. As a result, there was a second round of Vietnam casualties; in the years since the war's end, tens of thousands of veterans have died from suicide, drug and alcohol addiction, careless accidents, and diseases contracted in Vietnam. Countless survivors have done well, even prospered. But a sizable contingent have had trouble keeping a job, holding a marriage or relationship together, or even finding a home. The homeless veterans sleeping on the streets of large American cities bear witness to the stress and adjustment problems that prevent the emergence of healthy myths and that preclude the completion of healing rituals.

This book joins the distinguished company of Lifton's *Home From the War* and Hellman's *American Myth and the Legacy of Vietnam*, both of which comment on the mythological aspects of the conflict and its combatants. It is this type of book that needs to be read and re-read by health care professionals who work with combat veterans. It is this type of book that needs to be read by veterans themselves and discussed with their peers, their loved ones, and anyone else who has offered love, understanding, or support. In my work with the Olympia Foundation, I have seen U.S. Vietnam veterans and Russian veterans of the Afghanistan War compare experiences and share their memories of horror, their recollections of disenchantment, and their feelings of isolation.

Walking the Point contains any number of useful suggestions. Dr. Paulson's counsel is practical, sensible, and liberating. It is written by someone who has been there and has returned, someone who has been wounded and has healed, someone who has "walked the point" and has come back.

Stanley Krippner, Ph.D.
Professor of Psychology
SAYBROOK INSTITUTE
San Francisco, California

PREFACE

Several years ago I read an essay by Daryl Paulson on the experience of the Vietnam veteran as explained in terms of mythic themes of male initiation and the hero's journey. I was impressed with the essay and looked forward to its elaboration in book form. My high expectations for the book were more than rewarded. Paulson's *Walking the Point* is a stunning achievement. It presents an account of the war in Vietnam that is at once intensely personal and dispassionately wise. It is a book that needs to be widely read. I know of no other book that brings so much light and healing to our experience in Vietnam.

Paulson fought as a marine in Vietnam and, like so many other veterans of that war, suffered severe psychic injury from the nightmare of death in which he participated. Paulson tells his own story and the hauntingly similar stories of other veterans of the war. But Paulson's book is not just a weaving of personal narratives. It is a powerful account of the effect of Vietnam on the psyches of the men who fought in the war. *Walking the Point* follows the soldier's experience as it unfolded through the call to duty, the initiations of bootcamp and early field experiences, the brutal encounter with the enemy, and the return home. Paulson shows how these stages of the soldier's experience are stages of a transformative process of mythic magnitude: the hero's journey. All wars observe the stages Paulson discusses. What is distinctive of Vietnam is that it did not allow the hero's journey to be brought to a meaningful culmination. The war in Vietnam was without evident purpose for those who fought in it, and the return home was the very opposite of a hero's welcome. In consequence, the process of meaningful transformation was aborted, and many soldiers were left with psychic injury without any hope of healing or growth.

Paulson tells what it was like for a young man called to duty in Vietnam to lose his old identity, to be trained to kill and not be killed, to succumb to a vicious hatred of the enemy, to regress to primitively violent forms of mentality and behavior, to experience deep bonding with comrades, to become open to psychic and spiritual possibilities, and to be devastated in returning from a war that no one wanted to acknowledge. Paulson shows us how the trauma, guilt, and sense of meaninglessness experienced by many Vietnam veterans led them to drinking and drifting. Many veterans were unable to integrate their experience by finding a place for it within a meaningful life story and consequently were unable, upon returning home, truly to return to life. These veterans, rather than healing, fell prey to alcoholism and rootlessness, to fugitive wandering from job to job, relationship to relationship, or town to town. Unable to deal with who they were and what they did in the war, they fled above all from themselves, thereby condemning themselves to a kind of limbo. There are still many such veterans among us. Paulson's book is written especially for them. Paulson offers such veterans both a way of finding meaning in their experience and specific advice about how they can begin to heal their wounds.

But Paulson's book speaks not only to Vietnam veterans. It speaks to the entire generation of people who fought in or protested the Vietnam war. When Paulson was in the Marine Corps in Vietnam, I was in college participating in the antiwar movement. Had Paulson and I met back then, we would have been on opposite ends of the political spectrum. We would not have understood each other, and we probably would not have liked each other. Having read Paulson's book, I am now able to understand his younger Marine Corps self. Moreover, I have real compassion for that young man. I also have immense respect for the Daryl Paulson of today, the man who has written *Walking the Point*. He is a person of both wisdom and kindness. He blames no one for the events of the war. He is uncompromsingly honest about his own role in the war, and he helps his readers better understand the roles they played during the Vietnam years. *Walking the Point* is a healing book. It helped me heal my memories of Vietnam. It will help everyone else who reads it, too, especially veterans of the war who still have not finished the return home.

Michael Washburn, Ph.D.
Professor of Philosophy
INDIANA UNIVERSITY, South Bend

1
BEGINNINGS

"Being a man and being a Marine means
you must never give up."
—Staff Sergeant Turner, Marine Drill Instructor 1966

"The more you sweat in peace, the less you bleed in war."
—U.S. Marine Corps slogan

Certain roles and responsibilities in our culture have been traditionally male. Being the breadwinner—strong and enduring—and, of course, being the warrior or soldier were prevailing American values just twenty years ago. However, we Americans have witnessed the erosion of those traditional areas of male dominance due largely to the women's movement. Lacking the physical strength of men, women have used the justice system, their intelligence, and their authentic attributes to gain deserved liberation from male domination. Women have successfully challenged men in most professions; today, hardly any endeavor is a purely male one. The exception is the role of front line combat infantryman/warrior, which will certainly change after women's successful participation in the Persian Gulf War. Although many women currently serve in various capacities in the military, the role of warrior—the ground fighter—is still the domain of men, as it has been throughout the ages. As such, this story pertains to men, specifically to the combat veteran.

Over the course of history, men have had to live up to

rigid expectations, both implicit and explicit. In the 1950s, we were to be physically strong, mentally tough, and emotionally stoic. As a result of the feminist movement, many men who deplored the situation in Vietnam began to develop a softer, "feminine" side. This trend continued through the late '60s and into the '70s. I think that the '80s and early '90s have left many men struggling to find themselves. We were provided ideals in the '50s by our fathers and grandfathers; we were provided ideals in the '60s and '70s by women; but now we ask, "Who and what are we, and what do we really want?" In short, we find ourselves in a full-blown identity crisis.

Writers Robert Bly and Sam Keen have explored this dilemma in detail. Bly uses the metaphor of the "wild man" searching for his essence. I concur with Bly to some degree, but I wish to explain what men are looking for a little less poetically. I think this male dilemma begins in childhood with a variety of confusing—and sometimes adverse--influences. While our mothers did not want us to play with toy guns, roughhouse, have adventures in the backyard pond looking for toads, or be reckless and daring on our bicycles, our fathers wanted us to be tough and take responsibility—traits which they thought would ensure qualities of strength, endurance and competence. Though these qualities were important, they often obscured growth compatible with true individual needs, desires and possibilities. As we grew, school, teachers and media (primarily television) bombarded us with images of the stereotypical man. I believe this inundation of influences caused us to grow away from our true selves and potentials and set an impossible standard for many men. The sad result was a generation of men in fear of the world, in fear of their own insights, and—worst of all—in fear of being themselves.

To compensate for this sad state of affairs, we learned to *control* our world; after all, a threatening place must be controlled if we are to survive.

This compulsion to control hounds many of us throughout our lives. We have learned that we must strive, struggle, claw and scheme, just to stay in the race. We firmly and truly believe other males are out to dominate us unless we dominate them, a situation which alienates us from ourselves. Not only do we ignore our real, innate individuality, we actually *over-develop* areas of little interest to us because we *should*. We create an idealized, fantasy image of who we should be and how we will achieve it.

The men's movement is centered on finding our real selves. What is the real self? The real self is that central, inner, driving force unique to each person, yet inherent in all. The identification of the real self allows us to develop our unique potential; to be in touch with our true feelings, thoughts, wishes and interests; to tap into our authentic inner resources; and to express ourselves and relate to others in a genuine way. In fact, it not only *allows*, but encourages, insists, and demands our authenticity.

This book is not designed as a treatise on men's growth, but as a guide for a select group of men and those who seek a better understanding of them. This book is for and about the Vietnam combat veteran.

The Vietnam combat veteran has a special place in the men's movement. This is because the veteran has not experienced positive meaning from the war. Driven into a war he did not want, then prevented from fighting it with the military aggressiveness necessary to win, he lost faith. In most cases, upon his return from the war, he was shunned by his civilian community as a warmonger and a baby killer, and shunned by his military support community, such as the Veterans of Foreign Wars, because he lost the war. Consequently, he was forced to hide his involvement in the war, thereby losing the much needed support essential for adjustment and re-entry into civilian life. In moments of solitude and reflection, he could find no meaning for his involvement in the war or for the needless butchering of his brothers in the endless fighting. How could he justify killing fellow human beings? He could not. So he became burdened with guilt.

As his fellow Americans protested the war and its cruelty, he became more and more burdened with guilt. Finally, this guilt grew into a feeling of utter worthlessness; he was a despicable human being. *What am I to do? Where can I go? How can I get there? Does anyone want to hear my troubles? Not then, not now. That war was twenty-five years ago. The war in the Persian Gulf had nothing to do with me.*

I struggled for more than twenty years to find answers to these questions. I searched in my heart and in the hearts of my brother veterans. I believe I have found a very effective way of dealing with these painful questions in a way in which healing can occur. It is a process of viewing the Vietnam war as a male initiation rite, one which—unfortunately for most veterans—has not yet been completed.

The manner in which I use initiation rites is not a ritualistic rite as seen in the old Roman Empire movies. Rather it is a process of leaving an old way or stage in life in order to enter a new way or stage. The rite serves as a bridge between the new and the old. Throughout history, the initiation experience was truly a physical ordeal, but for the Vietnam veteran, it is appropriate to think of the initiation experience as a psychological ordeal undertaken to gain understanding and positive meaning from life's experiences.

In ancient times, formal initiation rituals were used quite successfully as entry vehicles to new life stages. The initiatory rites were usually interwoven with a mythological story. These myths clearly explained to the initiate where he was, where he was going, and how he would achieve that goal. In short, it provided meaning.

In contemporary society, we have nothing that accomplishes these developmental transitions as did the ancient initiations. While puberty, high school and/or college graduation, marriage, and retirement are certainly transitions carrying some implicit psychological meaning, they are, for the most part, superficial social conventions.

Male initiation rites, those rites which help a male define his maleness, are sadly lacking in our culture. Our society has dictated a high degree of male conformity necessitating an increased denial of those very characteristics which make him *male*. Moreover, social perceptions of men and women as unisexual beings have weakened male development by suppressing aggression. To truly come into their own, men must move away from these negative perceptions of aggression.

Males need to re-own their masculinity and their *fierceness*; males need to know that their feelings of aggression are instinctive and natural. There is nothing wrong with them *or* their feelings.

I am primarily concerned with the unrecognized fierceness of the male. True, males need to relate emotionally to other men, to the women in their lives, and to their children. But it is also essential that men protect their territorial interests—physically, if so required.

War often brings this *need to protect* to the fore. In Vietnam, I think this was the case, in spite of the reluctance of most men to go to war. The political, social, philosophical and religious theories were no longer relevant. If someone breaks into your house and threatens to murder your children and rape your wife, the immediate concern is not an examination of right, wrong, fair or unjust. The immediate concern is to survive and to protect.

At this point, the police cannot help you; the laws cannot help you; only you can help you. The preparation for and execution of this kind of situation is linked to male fierceness. I am not suggesting a reversion to the "law of the jungle," but rather that one recognizes that the world is not a Garden of Eden; certain people will take advantage of others, given the opportunity, and many males feel the responsibility to stand up for themselves.

This is the case in war. Unfortunately, the Vietnam veteran was not able to fight with his full potential. He had to fight with his hands politically tied. Then when he came back to America, he was degraded as a baby killer, a warmonger and a savage. I liken the Vietnam veteran's psychological plight to that of a man who watched his children killed and his wife raped, but was unable to protect them. He would be tormented not only by the injustice done, but by his own inability to act on his family's behalf.

I think the best way to help the Vietnam veteran help himself—as well as to aid those who attempt to help him— is by placing his Vietnam combat experience into the context of an initiation rite. We need to journey together into the experiences of the combat veteran, both in Vietnam and upon his return home. We also need to examine how some veterans have made the Vietnam experience a positive one in their lives. This will provide a model for those still struggling.

Let us begin with viewing combat as an initiatory experience. Physical combat has been with humanity since the beginning of man. With all the technological advancements in warfare, it is still the common infantryman or "grunt" who fights the bulk of the war. It is the infantryman who must experience the physical, emotional and mental anguish of war: being sick, being wounded, facing the tension and anxiety of impending death, and dealing with the deaths of others on a daily basis. For the modern infantryman, like his predecessors, life will never again be the same. No longer can he dismiss death as an event far in the future. Even if he survived the war, he would know always that death is but an instant away. No matter where he is, no matter what job or position he may hold, no matter who he marries, no matter how financially secure he is, he will always know, deep in his heart, that life on this earth holds no permanence for him.

For the most part, his world view is contrary to the world view of his peers who did not experience combat, those who were not exposed to its brutal forces. For the non-combatant, death is deniable; for the combat veteran, it is an overshadowing truth. While the non-combatant's world view is generally very predictable—graduation from high school, entering college, marrying, raising a family, working, and ultimately enjoying life in retirement—the combatant's world view usually is one of living in an unpredictable world which is undergoing constant, threatening change. He has seen so much death, so much suffering, and has been forced to live so closely with insecurity that he can no longer feel secure. Often the veteran's life has no meaning, no purpose, and no direction, once he has experienced war.

This meaningless state can be corrected with the positive use of mythology and initiation rites. In a number of mythological sagas, the initiate/warrior/hero was 1) "called" to enter the adventure, 2) began the "journey," 3) completed a series of "adventures," and 4) upon completing these adventures, gained greater knowledge and wisdom which could then be applied to his daily life. However, the predominant problem with the modern Vietnam combat hero was that the knowledge he gained from the war was not recognized or respected by either his culture or himself. Ironically, he completed the combat initiation experience but did not know it held the key to an initiation into a larger life, one that holds potential meaning for his life.

In this book, I shall espouse the theory that, by participating in the Vietnam war, the Vietnam combat veteran participated in an initiation rite. For him, accepting this theory may be central to his making positive psychological gains. If he does not do this, a perpetual, existential crisis will exist, that is, life will have no meaning for him.

Intense feelings of despair, stemming from lack of positive meaning from their combat experience, is a recurring situation faced by many Vietnam veterans with whom I have worked. In other words, they are convinced that there was and is nothing useful to be derived from the war. They feel, as do most Americans, that the United States did not win any political, economic or strategic victory. It only killed many of its young men.

The purpose of this work is to present a valid and useful approach to helping combat veterans who served in the Vietnam war. The majority of combat veterans were unprepared for the psychic trauma they experienced; this included being torn from the secure fabric of their community and fighting a war for an unknown purpose. The lack of psychological support from their country while serving in Vietnam was painful and traumatic, but being attacked, put down and protested against by their peers for involvement in Vietnam was excruciating.

The story of one veteran friend of mine, Joe, clearly defines this situation. Joe had grown up on a farm in Kentucky and was a peaceful, laid-back farm boy. After high school graduation, he worked on his father's farm and was preparing to marry his high school sweetheart. But Joe was also a poor boy, unable to get a draft deferment. Thus, shortly after graduation, he was served a draft notice. Joe had absolutely no desire to go to Vietnam, but he felt a moral responsibility to defend his nation from attack, so he joined the U.S. Army. He was drafted into an army infantry division and sent to Vietnam just in time for Christmas. There he learned about the horrors of war. He learned what it was like to see comrade after comrade killed. One moment, they would be laughing and joking with him with a twinkle in their eye about what they would do when they left Vietnam. The next moment, they would be dead, lying in the grass or mud with a poncho covering them until they were picked up by a chopper and taken to "Graves Registration." His friends were now cold and gray-looking, their eyes staring vacantly upward.

Joe ultimately survived Vietnam and was exuberant about going home and marrying his sweetheart, who had waited for him. Upon his return, however, things were not the same. The sweet smell of the summer's clover no longer made him glad to be alive. His sweetheart no longer brought him joy and happiness. He was now burdened with unfinished business. Every night the faces of his dead buddies visited him in his dreams. He saw their gray, cold faces with open eyes staring out into space. He was in pain. His sweetheart turned away from him, marrying a guy she had been seeing while he was in Vietnam. His parents kicked him off the farm for his drinking. He tried college in Louisville, but was seen by many as a warmonger. Within four months of starting college he dropped out, beginning a clouded, ten-year ordeal of running from himself, drifting from town to town and bar to bar.

This story, while unique to Joe, is similar to the stories of other veterans. While our past cannot be altered, we *can* begin to make sense out of our Vietnam experience. We *can* turn our lives around.

Our approach will be to re-frame or re-focus our feelings of despair and hopelessness and find positive meaning in the war experience. As previously stated, from the beginning of humanity, mythology has helped us make sense of our lives. In this context, veterans using mythology can discover who they are, where they are going, and where they fit in. That is, they can put meaning into their lives.

Meaning operates not only *in* our conscious awareness, but *outside*, as well. The meaning carried outside our awareness has a powerful effect on how we feel, think and act. The way in which we act or live may be thought of as our "personal mythology." In this sense, myths are not just stories, but constellations of beliefs, feelings and behaviors organized around a central core or theme; these constellations can help or hinder us in comprehending our lives in meaningful ways and in feeling connected with the universe.

Many mythological motifs portray the warrior "hero"

as having to proceed through the initiation experience alone. To a great degree, the Vietnam combat veteran also had to deal with *his* experience alone. He left his community alone. He endured combat training alone. He contended with pre-combat anxiety alone. Alone, he dealt with his thoughts of being killed in battle. He proved his worth to his combat unit alone. No one cheered him upon his return; he was again alone. Being alone, then, is something with which a combat veteran can identify. Since our society will probably never welcome him home or provide meaning for his involvement in the war, he must strive to gain a personal meaning from the war, a meaning unique to each warrior.

Personal meaning is possible, especially when viewed as a male initiatory rite. Jungian psychologists have long known that when one is told a mythological story, he often can stand away from it *psychologically*, extracting and incorporating some personal meaning into his life from the myth. For our purpose, myths will be viewed as stories which provide meaning to our past, a purpose to our present, and a positive direction for our future.

We will begin our journey, using myths as a basis for our work. Three recurring themes will be discussed in this work:

- ♦ the call to adventure,
- ♦ the initiation, and
- ♦ the return.

The call to adventure—the separation phase—consists of leaving the known behind and entering the adventure, or new dimension, in life. The initiation phase is the actual series of life events that one must experience before passing into the new dimension of life. The return is experienced only after a successful initiatory passage into the new developmental stage of life. The experiences and knowledge gained from this journey are passed on to others in order to aid them in their lives.

For example, let us look at the ancient male puberty rite. Prior to the call, both boys and girls generally helped the mother with domestic chores around the campsite. When boys entered the puberty phase of their lives, they were "called" or separated by the tribal men to be initiated into manhood. In this case, separation was usually drastic. Tribal men would come and physically seize the boys from their mothers. The boys entered an initiatory period where they were stripped of their formal identities and forced to endure initiatory brutalities, such as having certain teeth knocked out, being tattooed, or being circumcised. Through this process, they were accepted as one of the men, which was a major social advancement. Now they were the hunters, the ones who provided food for the tribe. They "returned" to the tribe as men, where they could tell others of the experiences and the insights gained from the initiatory ordeal.

The combat veteran also experienced the call, initiation and return. Let us now focus on his call to the adventure, his separation from his known life.

2
THE CALL

"Hell no! We won't go!"
—Protest slogan, march on the Pentagon, 1967

"When I go to Vi-etnam, I'm gonna kill some Vi-et Cong!
Sound off, 1-2! Sound off, 3-4! 1-2-3-4,3-4!"
—Marine bootcamp
marching song, 1967

*T*he country was split. On one side were the hippies, who were not only against the war, but at the very heart of American society's peace movement. On the other side were the mainstream Americans, referred to as the "silent majority." A young man growing up during that period was in a no-win situation. If he ran to Canada to avoid the draft, he would have to abandon his country and be labeled a traitor; if he went to the war in Vietnam, he risked death. I interviewed one of the men who chose to go to Canada during this period. Jeff had "refused the call for the military adventure," but heeded the call for his own adventure. Jeff graduated from high school in the spring of 1966 and entered college that fall. He was interested in pursuing a business administration career. He was deeply in love with a classmate, and he never doubted that she would eventually be his wife. Jeff and Molly spent all sorts of time together—enjoying school, playing frisbee on campus, hugging and kissing—just being together. Jeff never seriously considered having to join the military; that was for the others—the

11

poor or the dumb ones. As fate would have it, one-and-a-half years into Jeff's college career, his father died of a heart attack, ending his financial support. Because so many young men were in college at that time, using college deferment to avoid the draft, Jeff could find no student aid. As a last resort, he got a part time job to support himself, but flunked out of college. Within three months, he was drafted. Jeff could not envision himself killing anyone or, worse yet, being killed in a war fought on the other side of the earth for a reason not known to him. His brother and mother encouraged him to join the Coast Guard to avoid combat; he tried, but they were no longer accepting enlistments. Jeff's girlfriend wanted to get married and let it all work out, but her father, a World War II veteran, urged him to serve his country. He said it was Jeff's duty.

Jeff anxiously watched the Huntley-Brinkley news report nightly. He watched young soldiers tell of the fierce battles they fought and the body counts they attained. He listened to reports of the number of Americans killed; he heard the arguments for and against the war. He believed that he had to get out of the country. He just could *not* fight this war. It was too much. He left his mother, his brother and his girlfriend and went to Canada. He paid dearly for what made sense to him, encountering another initiatory experience, which was certainly no easier. Jeff's story, however, is not our real focus; ours is that of the combat veteran's separation.

I shall begin with my own situation. During my senior year in high school, 1966, I was deeply infatuated with a girl who really did not care about me. I was discouraged over my lack of success with her, bored with school, and could see no reason to go to college. I was unskilled in any kind of trade, such as carpentry or auto mechanics. I felt a sort of "power" telling people I was thinking of joining the Marine Corps after graduation.

If I did not go to college, I would be drafted. My peers perceived this as the ultimate failure. To be drafted was in the category of being a bum, and bums were used as "cannon fodder" in Vietnam. Successful men would let the unsuccessful fight the war. At the time, however, that perception did not bother me.

In February of 1966, I saw the John Wayne movie,

"Green Berets," and was intrigued by the adventure. I saw a way to escape my boredom. Since Russia and China were aggressively helping North Vietnam, I believed that World War III would be starting any time and that I might as well face the end fighting instead of hiding. There was also the glee of defiance. I could finally show my parents, my teachers and my fantasy girlfriend that I was tough and did not need them. So I joined the Marine Corps on the 120-day delayed program. That is, I joined the Marine Corps with four months of high school to complete before graduation. Ten days after high school graduation, I found myself getting ready to go to the Marine Corps Recruit Depot, San Diego, California, for boot camp.

My best and most beloved friend, Art, had a different story. He had been in and out of trouble with the local police, and finally, with the federal government. He and a friend had spray-painted a federal hydroelectric dam with 25 obscene words. Since Art had repeatedly been in trouble with the law, the judge gave him a choice: join the military or go to jail. He chose the Marine Corps.

Dave was a hippy residing in the Haight-Ashbury district of San Francisco in 1967. He had dropped out of his Wisconsin community and gone underground to avoid the draft and to experience free love, flower power and the assortment of drugs that went with the movement. However, he realized he was not living his life according to his inner dictates, so he went back home to his parents to face what he termed his "unfinished responsibilities." Since he had been served his draft notice eleven months earlier, he felt his going to Vietnam was highly probable. He and his father had a long discussion about living according to one's values and being responsible for one's life. Dave felt he had an obligation to serve his country, but he did not want to die. His father told him it had been the same during World War II. Not a lot of men really wanted to go; they went only out of a sense of duty. So Dave went to the draft board, told them what he had done, and waited for his sentence. They did nothing to punish him, but they inducted him into the Army for two years. He quickly changed this to a four-year enlistment in the Navy. Dave never wanted to go, never had a desire to kill. He went of his own inner dictate and feeling of moral responsibility to society.

Most of us who joined or were drafted into the military had a vague sense of apprehension, but the experience was still weeks or—at least—days away. There was still time to party and play a tough role with our friends.

I doubt that any of us realized just what was in store for us, and as we got closer and closer to the Marine Recruit Depot, I noticed our joking and laughing became less and less frequent and intense. That we were now in the United States military was becoming reality. It was no longer an abstract concept. Right now, we were owned by the government, by the Marine Corps; it could do with us what it chose for our entire enlistment. For us, this realization was very sobering. Our lives, as we knew them, were over. What would be next? What would military life be like?

As I looked out of the 727 Delta airliner on our landing approach to San Diego, I made a commitment to myself that although I was unsure of what lay ahead, I would not screw up. Then we landed. As soon as we got off the plane, we were loaded into buses and driven to the Marine Corps Recruit Depot (MCRD), where we reported for duty. So far, things were not so bad, and since it was about 2:30 a.m., we were directed to a temporary staging area where we could sleep until morning.

That morning I woke up to the peaceful whine of a small propeller-driven aircraft cruising through the air overhead. I was in a state between sleep and being awake, and since I grew up near an airport, I felt as though I was at home listening to an airplane. Abruptly, I was brought back to reality when a drill instructor marched into the squad bay yelling, "Get the hell out of the racks, you pukes! You goddam maggots!" He started yanking recruits out of their bunks yelling, "This ain't no picnic, girls! Get the fuck up!"

We were dumbfounded. What was he talking about? What were we supposed to do? Two more drill instructors came into the squad bay, also yelling and screaming about what miserable-looking pukes we were.

A hippyish recruit next to me had a scraggly beard, with which a drill instructor became obsessed. He walked over to the recruit, pulled his beard and told him if he did not have it gone in fifteen minutes, he would set it on fire with his cigarette lighter. Then he dragged him out of the room to the barber shop. He yelled for the rest of us to follow him down the stairs to the courtyard to have our hair cut. One at a time, we sat in the barber chair and had all our hair shaved off. It took about nine seconds to get a Marine Corps haircut. Then we were told to line up and get a shower in the receiving barracks next door. There, 87 of us were instructed to remove everything we were not born with and place it in the plastic sacks provided. We were then issued a small bar of soap each and marched naked to a communal shower. All 87 of us were cramped into a shower stall facility which would comfortably have held about 12 men. But the drill instructors kept yelling and screaming, "Shower up! Assholes to belly buttons, girls, get your asses in there and get cleaned up!"

After showering, we were issued underwear, socks, tennis shoes, a sweat shirt, utility trousers and a utility cap. We had no identity now. We could not recognize each other. We had no individuality, no sense of identity, and no contact with the outside world. We were totally separated from our communities, parents, friends, wives and girlfriends. Looking at each other without ever talking, our eyes asked: *What have we gotten into?*

Over the next several weeks, our spirits were broken. We were constantly humiliated and harassed. Finally, we lost our ability to care. We were dead to our past lives; they were but long ago dreams. We had no hopes or aspirations beyond just getting through the moment. Clearly, we were experiencing what is known in mythology as the "Dark Night of the Soul."

After about three weeks of living in dread and despair, however, we began to identify with the Marine Corps. It seemed as if we had had no other life, as if we had always been in bootcamp. We noticed that the drill instructors also began to change their attitude toward us. We were now called "men" and "Marines" instead of "girls," "pukes," or "scum," and we began to live up to it. We learned to march; we learned to fight; we learned to work together. We were preparing for our own initiation experience, that of combat as a unit, as a military machine.

3
INITIATION

"It is more dangerous driving America's highways then going to Vietnam."
—1965 quote from a non-Vietnam veteran

"We've got to get out of this place, If it's the last thing we ever do!"
—Animals, 1964, theme song of the Vietnam veteran

*O*nce we completed our infantry training, we were destined for South Vietnam. Although we had not actually experienced combat, we thought we had a pretty good idea of what we were getting into. We had heard war stories from returning veterans. We had viewed report after report on the nightly news. We had seen trauma after trauma in movies with actual combat footage, but we were in the pre-combat stage of the initiation experience. We were committed to the adventure, and there was no turning back. We, the mythological heroes, stood alone in this adventure. This was a time when we thought about dying, about leaving our parents and loved ones, and about going to a foreign country to lay down our lives for America.

It was a time when I started talking to God. I had had to go to church and Sunday school all my life, and I had pretty well ignored the whole thing. Now, however, faced with the very real possibility of dying in Vietnam, I started to talk to God. I had a conception of God being a wise old man sitting on a giant, gold throne. I told him I would

protect the United States from attack and do a good job—
so good that he would be proud of me.

Over and over, I wondered how it would be to really
experience combat. Was there a lot of shooting or just a
little? What was it like to be mortared? Rocketed? Was it
non-stop, 24-hour fighting? Could I kill another human
being? If I could not, would I be hanged as a traitor? If I
were killed, would my body be lost? Would it be mutilated?
Would anyone remember me?

I even dreamed about combat. Dreaming I was walking
on patrol, I found that it was not so bad, just as Sergeant
Rock of the comic book found it.

One friend of mine decided to go on a perpetual party
and drink his fear away. As we waited to go, he would
"party hearty" as he called it, for it was his last chance.

We did not have much time to dwell on how combat
might be, for we were flown to Vietnam very quickly. A
four-day layover in Okinawa, and then we were sent on to
Da Nang Air Base where we were immediately assigned
our in-country units. We certainly had doubts about our
performance in combat, but our morale was fueled by our
training in boot camp. We definitely felt that we had control
over our combat destiny—whether we lived or died. Our
thoughts were based on our boot camp logic: if we did
everything we were told and did not screw up, we would
live; if not, we would be shipped home in a body bag,
dead. However, we were scared to death. Then the day
came—the day we had to go on combat patrol.

Many of us were killed during this period, because of
our inexperience in combat, but for those of us who
survived our first experiences of combat, a psychological
transition occurred: total despair.

In my first two weeks of combat, our radio man was
shot through the head just in front of me, while on patrol.
He had moved into the path of a bullet destined for me. He
was talking to another unit, and then it was over. He was
gone. Just like that. He was simply "tagged" and "bagged,"
that is, he was identified by his unit and put in a body bag
to be sent home. Just like that. I saw seventeen of my
comrades who were coming in on a helicopter for a ground
assault killed by a direct hit of a 121 mm rocket—all killed.
Just like that! At the end of those two weeks, I watched six

seasoned veterans destroyed by an incoming mortar round as they ate their C-rations. Just like that, they were gone. They were tagged and bagged. From my standpoint, combat was far too ruthless, random and absolute for me to be able to predict or prevent my death.

In classical mythology, this portion of the initiation was referred to as the Road of Trials. It was during this period that the hero was severely tested. I, too, was tested during the 13-month ordeal, by continually witnessing young friend after young friend brutally killed, and by killing Viet Cong and North Vietnamese Army (NVA) members as if they mattered no more than rats, gleefully enjoying their suffering and pain. I was becoming progressively numb to my humanness by living this life. Soon there was no boundary between the war and myself. Now we were enmeshed, the war and I—united in this senseless butchering. My proud motto became, "Kill all the gooks, let God sort the fuckers out!" I had become a true killing machine.

I recall an incident at the An Hoa Combat Base in 1969 around the TET offensive. One night—and it was at night when so much of the actual fighting occurred—we were hit by an NVA force. They attacked and overran a portion of the compound. About 35 NVA had broken into the camp and were looking for the communications bunker to blow up. We bounced hand flares into the night sky to see them. We laid down a massive barrage of .223 caliber rifle fire, .30 caliber machine gun fire and rocket-propelled grenades. At one point, we were supported by a .50 caliber machine gun located on the main observation tower. Very quickly we killed every one of the NVA and shredded them into what looked like hamburger. That is how massive our fire power was against the group.

The next morning, we went over to the NVA bodies and took turns taking pictures of our kill. It was a joyous time. We had "kicked ass," and we felt good about it. We had a body count delivered to our doorsteps. We scraped up the hamburger-like bodies and laid the chunks and bits and pieces along the main road to the camp. It was a warning to the Vietnamese people who were working on the compound filling sand bags not to betray us. This was a time when we wished we could kill every one of the Vietnamese. That would solve our problem. It is incredible that we could have regressed to such a primitive way of functioning in such a short time. Life had no value except the saving of our own.

Still, during times alone, I wondered just what I had gotten myself into. I knew I was in a situation way over my head. What I was doing and how I was doing it somehow did not seem right. I was so terrified that I would never again see a friendly face, a face of one who would care about me and not try to kill me. I knew I was deeply, emotionally wounded, but I was determined to survive at all costs or, at least, kill as many NVA as I could before I was killed.

Since I was new to combat and ignorant of the actual ways of combat, I knew that I would not survive for long. I prepared to accept my death as well as I could. As I have said, I clearly saw that it did not matter how proficient I was; a random rocket or mortar hit could end my life in an instant. This was not an abstract threat of tomorrow or next week; it was 13 months of "now"—thirteen months of wondering if I would be alive to eat the next meal, to see the next sunrise or the next sunset. I began hoping that since I would surely die, I would get it over soon, rather than prolonging my suffering through the end of my tour. This, I found later, was a prominent attitude among the infantrymen.

In mythological motifs, the hero experiences an encounter with what is called the father figure. The father figure was psychologically important in these stories because he was the force who fiercely guided the hero through the trying times of the initiation. The father image, his guidance and his strength, were also present for us. After having proven ourselves worthy (still alive after a number of battles), we were "taken in" by a more experienced combat veteran, "the father." This person acted as our guide and took an active role in teaching us to survive combat.

A leathery old Marine took an interest in me and taught me how to survive. He taught me the laws of combat; I learned the sound differences of incoming and outgoing mortars and rockets, and I mastered the art of "walking point" without being killed or getting the entire squad killed. In Vietnam, walking the point was dangerous. It meant one walked 25 to 50 meters in front of the rest of the patrol. It meant the point man was the first to get shot, step on a booby trap, or set off a mine. To me, it was an exhilarating experience that not just anyone could do. I had to be prepared and tested for walking the point by "the father." If I failed the test, I would be swiftly killed. If I passed, I was one with the father; I was competent and potent.

I remember vividly the first time I walked the point. I felt a strong connection to the NVA. I had to pit my survival skills against theirs. There was no one to hide behind or to take lessons from now. It was an exhilarating, yet terrifying, experience, knowing that death could come to me or the entire squad at any given moment if I failed.

In addition—like the heroes in mythology—after suffering and enduring and surrendering to apparent utter failure, we were assisted by supernatural forces. For me, this assistance came in the form of "intuition." I actually began to feel warnings about dangerous situations before they occurred. I was truly amazed at how these extra "survival senses" seemed to develop as I needed them.

For example, during the 1969 TET offensive, I was again at the An Hoa Combat Base with my unit, awaiting helicopter transportation to a very hot, bloody battle taking place in an area called Elephant Valley. Elephant Valley was a treacherous place, and we dreaded going there. I was very preoccupied with what kind of shit (combat) was going on there, but the weather was bad and we could not go that night. I had a very strong feeling of impending danger while lying in my tent. I could not sleep, my heart raced, my anxiety escalated, and a voice inside me said, *Leave the tent, now!* I gathered my flack jacket, helmet, ammunition and poncho, and I walked to the perimeter trenches, where I tried to sleep. About two hours later, our compound was overrun by NVA. During this attack, our camp was pounded with hundreds of high explosive rockets and mortar rounds. The ground shook from the impact of these rounds; a series of violent fire explosions engulfed the entire northern side of the compound. We thought we would never survive the night, as we repelled wave after wave of NVA attackers. Finally, by morning, they retreated.

I was so tired and sore that I limped back to my tent to sleep. When I got there, I was shocked to discover a huge hole in the tent, directly in line with the spot where my head usually rested on my cot. A boulder, approximately three feet across, lay on top of what was left of my cot. That boulder would have killed me had I stayed in the tent. From that time on, I depended on supernatural aid to keep me alive. Time and time again, intuition assisted me in surviving the initiation of war.

Superstition was common in the infantry. A lucky rock, chain or saying made the difference in whether one *thought* he would live or die. One of my friends carried an empty beer can that Raquel Welch supposedly drank from during "The Bob Hope Christmas Special" at Da Nang. As long as he had that can and could hold it to his chest, he was safe. Another friend felt he had to write in his journal every day. If he missed a day, he was in danger. Another person, from Tennessee, wore a raccoon tail on his helmet. He felt that as long as he had that amulet, he would be spared. Yet another felt that if he did not eat the pound cake in the C-ration can, he would be spared. He had seen too many people killed after eating the pound cake; it was a bad omen.

Sometimes the supernatural aid almost made us shudder. At one time, we believed that we could control our destiny by "just trying harder." However, as we saw the gruesomeness, swiftness and finality of death, we thought we would never "make it"—never survive the combat. At some point in the initiation process, however, this changed. We began to see that you were not killed until it was your time. Our motto became, "When your number is up, you're wasted—but not a second before." This brought us some comfort. There was reason and purpose to the apparent random killing. We were part of a larger system and would now die only when it was our time. How could such a perceptual change have occurred? One would think mere chance was the arbitrator of life or death. The more shit (combat) you saw, the worse were your chances of surviving. This was how we first perceived it; but as we survived situations that were "unsurvivable," our perceptions changed. Let me explain this with some examples.

Larry, an army artilleryman, was in his tent with eight other men. Suddenly, his camp took five 121mm rocket hits. His tent took a direct hit, killing everyone in it but

Larry. He was not hit by any shrapnel. He was burned and had both eardrums ruptured, but that was it. The 121mm rocket, a very lethal weapon, is considered to have an absolute kill range of 50 meters. Larry had been about eight meters from the rocket crater. His number was *not* up.

Jeremy was a driver of a large tow truck which accompanied convoys in case any of the vehicles got stuck in the muddy, back convoy trails. On one trip, his truck hit a mine, which was reported to be one of our 500-pound unexploded bombs. The impact blew the entire engine and cab off the hoist unit. He was blown into the air and landed about twenty meters away, in the soft, cushiony area of a rice paddy. Urinating in his pants, he suffered no wounds except to his pride. His number was not up either.

Another instance is from my combat experience. During the 1969 TET offensive, my unit, part of the 5th Marine Regiment, was camped at An Hoa, which was about 35 miles northwest of Da Nang. It was a horrible place, and NVA ran rampant. John B., John O. and I had survived the major area operations as members of "Task Force Yankee." Now this was over, and we were going back to the 1st Marine Division rear for a little rest and relaxation at China Beach.

Before going to China Beach, we were assigned to a work detail for several days at the 1st Marine Division headquarters. This was a welcome assignment, because it kept us out of the bush at An Hoa. On the second and last day of our detail before going to China Beach, I noticed that John O. and John B. were unusually moody. They were bitchy. How could this be? We were going to have some fun at China Beach. For lunch we ate some warm ham and cheese sandwiches and drank "cold" Coca Cola. This was the life—why could we not be office pogs (administrative personnel)? We laughed about them having it made. But I had a gut feeling that something was bothering John B. and John O. I asked them about it, and they responded that there was nothing wrong. I worked alongside them, folding tents, all afternoon, but there was some barrier between us. That night we were in the 1st Marine Division's Supply Office—supposedly a very safe place. I told John O. and John B. that the club opened at

7:00 p.m. and this would be our chance for some cold beer
and fun. In An Hoa, the beer we drank was hot and foamy.
Because of its consistency, it just would not stay down.
Here, at the club—a real club, a shack in which *cold* beer
was served—things could be different. Drinking would be
fun instead of an ordeal; it wouldn't be a struggle to keep
hot, foamy, biting beer settled in your stomach.

John O. and John B. were not interested! We had a
fight, and I stormed out of the office and headed to the
club. On my way, I heard an explosion. My heart
plummeted to my feet, for I knew it was incoming. When
I heard the second and third explosions, I ran for the lines.
I knew we were in trouble, even if the office pogs here did
not. Then the sirens went off. About an hour later I heard
that the Division Supply Office was hit and two marines
were killed. I wondered where John O. and John B. were;
I wondered who bought the ranch up there and kind of
laughed to myself that it served "them office pogs" right.
Then I heard that John O. and John B. were the ones who
were killed, and I was needed to identify them. I could
not. I just could not bear to see my two best friends,
destroyed. I had been closer to them than to any humans
on the planet. We had suffered together on patrols, been
through TET together, been drunk together, and relied on
each other to pull and force the other through combat, when
one of us could go no more. We had each been jilted by a
girlfriend; we shared this agony together. We had shared
hopes of going to college together, and now it was over.
They had been taken from me. From my pack I removed
the fifth of R&R we had planned to share at China Beach;
I drank and held back my tears and drank and held back
more tears—tears that would not be shed for six more
years—and drank and drank. Visualizing burying them
safely and lovingly in the deep blue sea, out of harm's
way—respectfully watching them peacefully descend to
sleep through eternity—brought me comfort in my sorrow.

The next morning I found out that both John O. and
John B. would have been safe had they not panicked and
run away from the bunker into an open room, where they
met the mortar round. To this day, I cannot explain why
two seasoned combat veterans ran from a bunker into a
room, separated from everyone in the office, to be killed.

They were the only ones killed. Truly, their numbers were up and mine was not.

These experiences were very powerful and brought us to a more peaceful, fatalistic stage. When your number is up, it's up. There is no death before that time.

The hero meeting the goddess is another mythological motif encountered in many tales. The meeting of the goddess occurs only after the hero has endured many trials and has proven himself worthy. The goddess' function is to provide the hero with both bliss and comfort. For me, once I came to terms with my combat situation and accepted it, I was free to just *be*. Gone were most of the fears of being killed, for now I accepted that if it was to be, it would be. I no longer felt responsible for survival. If I was killed, that was simply the way things were intended to be. My number was up.

Once the hero entered this stage, the actual initiation was nearing completion. He had survived everything the war could present to him and had not crumbled. It was during this period that the combatant felt most comfortable being an infantrymen. He was no longer an initiate; he was a full-fledged combat veteran.

4
THE RETURN

"You're not the same, any more. You're no fun."
—a friend to me in a bar back home

...so much is said about wasted lives..."
—T.S. Elliot, "The Wasteland"

"Judge not, that you be not judged."
—Matthew 7:1

*"Perish the day I was born... Why was I not
stillborn, why did I not die when I came out of
the womb? ...hedged in by God on every side."*
—Job 3:3-23

*F*or those of us who survived the "Nam," our day to
leave the country finally came. We were going back to the
WORLD—a name we gave the United States—home to
round-eyed, friendly, warm and affectionate women. Home
to a world where the streets were asphalt-paved and there
were flush toilets, hot and cold running water, food other
than C-rations, and plenty of cold beer.

Unlike the mythological hero who—after going through
the initiatory ordeal to find the gold, the golden fleece, or
the grail—brings back his trophy to share with all, the
Vietnam veteran brought back no treasure. That is, he
attained no positive knowledge (treasure) which he could
share with the others in his community. When our 707

landed at El Toro Marine Air Station, I was secretly preparing for a hero's welcome. I think all of us reasoned that we would get a doubly strong welcome because we had fought in spite of the absence of any explicit government plan to win the war. For example, congress and/or the president would decide to bomb North Vietnam one week, but stop bombing the next. This on-again, off-again strategy was terrible for our morale. We would often wonder, *Why the hell are we here if our leaders cannot make up their minds whether to fight the war or bail out?* Given these unusually hard conditions, we now thought we would be rewarded.

We landed and walked out of the plane to our homecoming reception. I saw *three* people waiting for us. That was it! They were Marine wives who had volunteered to serve cookies and Kool-Aid to us. Where was everyone else? Where were the women to welcome us home? They should be here, I thought.

Once in the air terminal, we were escorted to waiting military buses and driven to Camp Pendleton Marine Base for discharge or reassignment. During the drive, some college-age people screamed obscenities at us and flipped us the bird. I can still remember their yelling something about our being "warmongers."

At Camp Pendleton we were swiftly processed and bused to Los Angeles International Airport to schedule flights home. At the Los Angeles airport, I went to a bar to have a couple of drinks while waiting for my flight. This was an especially big event for me. It was my first legal drink in the United States and in a bar, for now I was of age, 21. I felt like being friendly, so I tried to start a conversation with two women sitting next to me, but they ignored me. Then I tried to talk to a couple of guys, but they, too, ignored me. It began to dawn on me that no one cared that I had served in the Vietnam war. I felt like a misfit.

The lack of care and concern for what I had been through was even apparent with my friends when I arrived home and went out drinking with them. Things were different. I noticed not only that they did not care about the war, but that I was now different from these guys. They were caught up in being "cool" and contriving to attract women. I just did not care. I had just seen hundreds of U.S. servicemen killed; I had also seen hundreds and hundreds of North Vietnamese soldiers killed and had tried to kill as many of them as I could. I had faced thirteen months of not knowing if I would die that day. Now, to worry about my hair or a woman seemed petty and meaningless. To protect myself from the meaninglessness of this life, I found a friend that night. It was a friend who would keep me calm and mellow for the next two years. That friend was Budweiser.

The first several weeks back in the states were also hard on me when I had to describe the Vietnam experience to my friends. After a friend asked me, I thought to myself, *How could I describe that* hell *in words?* I felt anger, frustration, fear and hate, all welling up inside of me. I felt like beating the table in utter frustration, but instead I calmly took another drink of beer, said, "It was real bad," and left it at that. But I knew—not only consciously, but to the center of my being—that something was terribly and painfully wounded within me. My friend did not really care. He was more interested in collecting information to support his anti-war beliefs. For me, however, it was different. He had opened up a huge wound inside me. I recalled the friends from my unit whom I saw killed—John O., John B., Jose, Peter, Jocko, Fraize, Rocko, Pork Chops and Glen. What had they died for? They died for nothing—nothing but bullshit. I took another drink of beer... and another... and another.

Other veterans had similar experiences. Joey, for example, went back to college and his fraternity when he returned. He found, however, that he was no longer wanted. The fraternity brothers no longer wished to associate with him. He was "flawed." He was a Vietnam veteran. He could not deal with that, so he shot himself in the head.

Art, a Marine Corps veteran, came back to the states and went to college. He suppressed his entire Vietnam experience and never spoke a word about it to his non-military friends. By these actions, he found that he was harboring tremendous amounts of guilt. To compensate for this, he tried to be all things to all people. He tried to be the best, most caring friend to the women he knew, and he tried to be the best, most caring friend to the men he knew. In the process, however, he denied his own needs. On the outside he put on a good show, but his inner conflict was betrayed by his ever present need for a drink, an R&R on the rocks.

As he continued to avoid himself and his inner needs, Art's guilt and inner conflict became worse. He compensated by being even nicer to the people he knew. Finally, under this self-imposed pressure, school became too much of a burden for him. He dropped out of school, left the country, and went to live in Cozumel, Mexico.

It was during his stay in Mexico that Art began to question his involvement in Vietnam. Had he screwed up? What if he really had not gone to defend the country? What if he had been wrong? He assuaged those questions with even more alcohol.

Art was not alone in this introspection. I think all of us veterans shared a sense of condemnation. We felt a kind of deep guilt which sent terror to the very core of our being. If we had been wrong about the war, were we not similar to Nazi criminals? Was there really a reason to keep on living? How could we live with ourselves, having seen and experienced all the brutalities of war and survived it, only to realize that our involvement served no positive purpose?

I sensed the overt damage within myself. I remember fantasizing about how warm and caring I would be when I got back from Vietnam. I would find that special woman and devote my life to our relationship. The entire time I was in Vietnam, I thought to myself how nice it would be to be held by a warm, loving woman, to watch her laugh and smile as I teased her. I would fantasize over and over what it would be like.

When I did return, things were different. I found that I did not really like to be with women; they made me nervous. To be held by a woman made me feel very vulnerable. Instead of feeling good, I would feel terribly sad and afraid in her arms. It was almost like being a little boy again, in need of a mother to hug away my pain. But I was 21 years old; I was too old to need a mother figure. Since these vulnerable feelings were, I thought, a sign of my weak character, I began avoiding any closeness with women.

I did find that I could get close to a woman when I drank. Drinking made relationships with women much easier; I did not feel vulnerable and could use them for sexual gratification. After all, what was a woman for, except to fuck? Many other veterans I talked with shared this experience. In fact, our new motto became, "Find them, feel them, fuck them, forget them." We had to distance ourselves from any meaningful encounter with women because we felt that we could not share with them what we had experienced. How could you tell your girlfriend what it was like for you to shoot another human being? How could you tell her how vulnerable and scared you had felt, never knowing if you would live another hour the whole time you were in Vietnam? How could you tell her what it was like to kick dead NVA soldiers because you were so angry at them for killing your friends? I was afraid to tell any woman what it was like.

How could I tell her about the horror I felt watching a dump truck taking the corpses of seventeen of my friends to be embalmed? How could I tell her what I felt when I watched their blood drip and flow from the tailgate onto the ground? How could I tell her how deeply I hurt, of the agony I was in, and how gnawing my suffering was? How could I tell her that the pain and guilt followed me like a beast tracking its prey? How could I tell her that the pain hounded me at night, during the day, and even while making love? What would she think of me if I told her? I feared that if any woman knew this about me, she would freak out, go into convulsions, vomit, and totally reject me for being such a disgusting human being. What was I to do? I did what seemed best: I drank and drank and drank.

So did most of the other veterans I knew, and since we drank so much and so often—while pretending it was partying—it was hard for others to recognize it as a way of masking our own pain. But God, it was there.

Then one day, it happened. I had an anxiety attack. I was sitting in an accounting class when I suddenly felt as though I were dying. My heart began to pound; I was becoming dizzy and my eyes would not focus. I began gasping for breath and sweating profusely. I began to "freak out." I walked out of class, pretending everything was okay, and went immediately to the student health service. There, however, the doctor who examined me could find nothing wrong with me. To me, this meant that something

very serious was wrong with me. I began to relive feelings
of being near death, as I had been in Vietnam. This totally
confused me.

After suffering about five more panic attacks and
running to the doctor, he sent me to a psychiatrist. I did not
relish the idea of having mental problems, but I needed to
be spared from this new form of suffering. When I saw the
psychiatrist, he disinterestedly asked me what my symptoms
were. I told him, and he prescribed two kinds of
tranquilizers, as well as an antidepressant, and told me to
take it easy. That was the last thing I could think of doing,
I was so distraught with my life. I tried, though. I tried to
enjoy target shooting with my .22 rifle, but I began to
physically shake so badly while aiming, I could not shoot.
Shooting had been my favorite pastime, and now it was
gone. I just could not endure it; it made me too tense.

I tried to go on relaxing picnics with my friends, but I
became too uneasy, even with the tranquilizers, to enjoy
the picnic. I kept feeling that someone—the enemy—was
hidden in the trees, stalking me, just as I had felt in Vietnam.
At times, I became so tense and anxious on the picnics that
I would have to drink a couple of belts of whiskey just to
get through the ordeal.

No fear impacted me as much as the fear I felt during
thunder storms. Even though I knew thunder was caused
by lightning, the sound of thunder would send me right
back to Vietnam. It felt as if I were undergoing a rocket
attack. I would have to drop to the ground to protect myself
from the incoming.

Other veterans I have talked to reported similar
experiences. They have reported panic attacks when a fire
alarm is set off, when a helicopter flies over them, and when
hearing loud noises. This period is pure hell for the veteran.
Initially, upon our return, we expected to have gained some
positive feelings from our Vietnam experiences. We found
instead that the quality of our lives was slipping fast,
especially as we began to experience panic with benign
events.

In mythological stories, after the hero had successfully
completed his initiatory experience, he returned to the world
to share his newly acquired knowledge with the common
people, in order to be of service to them. It was in this

situation that he was the hero. Yet, for the returning Vietnam combat veteran, there was nothing of value which he could share. There was only pain, frustration, and anguish. And instead of being treated as the hero, he was shunned by his friends for being a veteran; he was shunned by the World War II and Korean veterans for losing the war, by the hippies for being a warmonger, and by himself for allowing himself to be duped by his country. Vietnam was not a war to save the enslaved Vietnamese people; it was not fought to protect America. It was a cruel joke and a cruel turn of fate for the veterans who fought it. It seemed just one more thing that he had screwed up in his life.

Faced with the agony that there was no positive meaning (or Grail) to be found in participation in Vietnam, I was thrown into an existential crisis. My entire world began to collapse. I could only suffer and drink and suffer and drink and suffer and drink. My world continued to fall apart, as I realized and felt to my core that my involvement in the war was for no positive purpose. Over and over in my mind, I lamented how I had trusted the government and it had betrayed me. Over and over, I asked myself, how could the politicians have done this to us?

Plagued with guilt, I tried to find a place where I could go for forgiveness, to get away from this hell. I felt too guilty to go to God and church, for I had killed, I had injured, and I had tortured my fellow human beings with intense delight. No, I could not go to God or church, for I had too much blood on my hands. I reasoned that no one wanted me now, not even God, for I had killed His children.

I felt completely alone and totally isolated. I lived in an alien world with which I could not communicate. I did not fit in with the other college students, since I was a Vietnam veteran, but I did not fit in with the military, either. I spent a little of my time studying, but most of my time I spent drinking to assuage the pain of life's all-too-obvious meaninglessness. The recurring visions and dreams of the killing I had seen and the killing I had done began to intensify. I just could not stop visualizing—and reliving— the emotional scenes of my comrades' deaths. Even the alcohol was not taking the edge off. I could not sleep, and I could not bear the pain of being awake. I could only suffer and hurt and despair over the meaninglessness and aloneness I endured, but even these were not as painful as the guilt.

One night, I found my way out. I looked at my loaded .38 caliber revolver with perverse pleasure, thinking that I could end it all. My suffering would be over in a flash, and I would have the last laugh. One 158 grain hollow-point in my brain, and it would all be over. But as I looked at my gun, I thought about the Biblical Job's suffering and how it had been for a purpose. Then I thought about my comrades who had been killed and the despair they would feel with no one to tell their story. I started to cry and then decided to stay drunk until I found a psychotherapist who could help me. For the next year and a half, I remained mostly drunk. Incredibly, though, I finished college and went to work for my father. Even more incredible, I got married. However, the marriage made me feel so guilty, because I did not love the woman, that it made me seek out a psychotherapist in earnest. This time I found the one I was looking for, one who not only knew psychotherapy, but who cared about me as a person.

Returning to mythology, we note that, unlike the mythological hero, the Vietnam hero's return was not his physical return from the war. When he returned physically, he had one more obstacle with which to contend in the initiation process. This is a critical point. The vast majority of people, veterans included, think that the physical return from Vietnam was equivalent to the "return" of the hero in mythology. Hence, the majority of veterans to this day are in a sort of limbo. They are in a hellish state, caught between a war that is over and a society that does not care about their story, even though they need society's help in being reintegrated into the social fabric. The real return for most of us, then—if we had one—began only after we dealt with what we had done in Vietnam. That took place in the therapist's office.

5
THE ACTUAL RETURN

"When people see some things as beautiful,
other things become ugly.
When people see some things as good,
other things become bad."
—Tao Te Ching

"The Lord gave and the Lord has taken away.
Blessed be the name of the Lord."
—Job 1:21

"Go your way; and as you have believed
so let it be done for you."
—Matthew 8:13

*A*fter being back in the United States for some time,
many Vietnam veterans realized that they could no longer
escape their emotional agony through denial. They were
no longer in Vietnam, nor had they "returned" from the
war. They were stuck in a wasteland, in a pseudo-return.
As their pain affected more and more areas of their lives
negatively, they had to admit to themselves that they were
in deep trouble that was getting worse.

So many Vietnam veterans were caught in a dilemma.
How could they be brave, strong men if they could be
victims of emotional pain and suffering? To be a victim of
pain and suffering and to admit it was the equivalent of
being a pussy, or a wimp.

Chris, an army combat veteran, finally came to the end of his emotional rope. He could endure no more. The nightmares, the drinking, the drugs and his divorce drove him to seek help at the Veteran's Administration Center. There he was given a pep talk by a Veteran's Administration physician. He was told to stop feeling sorry for himself and to be thankful that he was not *really* wounded. To be really wounded, according to this doctor, meant to be physically wounded. Chris went home in total despair, feeling weak and worthless. He sat down on the porch, drank a beer, went to the woodshed and ended it all by shooting himself in the heart with a .45 caliber handgun.

For me, this period was, in many ways, more painful and traumatic than actual combat had been. During this time, I had to face the darker side of my personality, the side which had participated in the killing and maiming of other human beings and had witnessed the brutal killing of friend after friend.

Since I had had a very negative experience with a psychiatrist a few years before, I was in no frame of mind to trust another one. I remembered how cold and uncaring that psychiatrist had seemed, and how dehumanized and worthless I had felt from the encounter. I had felt like a giant rat whom the psychiatrist studied with indifference. My emotional pain mattered not at all to him, for it was only a biochemical imbalance. To protect myself from another psychological disaster, I tested and retested the new therapist to see if he merited my trust. Eventually I began to trust him and to deal with some of the war issues which plagued me.

I had to experience the war all over again; this time, emotionally, I had to face the various combat situations I had been holding in. I had to acknowledge that I had killed and had done it with great satisfaction. One major area of guilt for me was that I had tried to kill 21 NVAs as a personal birthday present to myself for my twenty-first birthday; having killed only 20 1/2, I was extremely upset. Someone else had finished off the twenty-first NVA for me, and I was credited with only one-half a body count for that one. In therapy, I had to experience the tremendous guilt of what I had done and the even greater guilt about how willing I had been to do it. I realized that had I been a German soldier in World War II, and had I been asked to gas Jewish prisoners, I unquestioningly would have done so. I would have justified it, thinking, *Our leaders know what is best.* In therapy, I recognized that I had never given any serious thought to what I was doing in Vietnam. I learned the need for responsibility. Even though I had given no thought to what I did in Vietnam while I was there, I was still responsible. With this realization, I was very remorseful. This position was very sobering, but while I was in the pit of my despair, something wonderful happened. I read about the writer of the religious hymn, "Amazing Grace." The writer had been a Negro slave trader who participated in many Negro slave killings before he experienced a religious conversion. The words of that hymn struck a deep chord in me, resonating within me to create deep feelings I had not experienced before.

> *Amazing Grace, how sweet the sound*
> *that saved a wretch like me!*
> *I once was lost, but now am found,*
> *was blind but now I see.*

I really identified with those words, not from a religious posture, but from a forgiving stance. I, too, felt like a wicked *wretch*, and I, too, could be forgiven. Realizing that, I began to ease up on myself and stop condemning myself so ruthlessly. I began to accept that I had not done a lot of noble things in Vietnam, but I had done the best I could do at the time and that I would not be a willing stooge again.

In one of my psychotherapy sessions, I described how John O. and John B. were brutally killed. Since I was so emotionally close to them, their deaths had a major impact on me. While describing to the therapist the death scene, it became as vivid as it had been when it was occurring. I could see the illumination flares burning all around me; I could smell the burned gun powder in the air; and I could feel the ripping pain in my heart when I was told my two best friends had just been killed. I began to cry in the psychologist's office and felt embarrassed, so I held my tears back as best I could. After the session, when I had to drive to a city about 100 miles away for a meeting, I let the tears come. As I drove down the highway, the agony and pain of losing my two friends re-surfaced. This time, I did not hold back. I cried and cried, for the entire 100-mile trip. When I got to the city, I was so drained from crying that I immediately checked into a motel and went to bed.

The next morning when I got up, there was an amazing change in my perception. I could smell breakfast cooking, and it made me feel peaceful and good, reminding me of when I was a young boy at home and my mother cooked me breakfast. Also, the people staying at the motel now seemed "friendly," though I did not talk to any of them. Even the birds who were gathered on the lawn seemed to be friendly. I felt alive. I felt connected to my body and connected to the universe. This was the beginning of my psychotherapeutic "cure" from Vietnam.

Mike, an Army infantryman, reported experiencing a similar situation. He came back to the United States and felt the rejection from his friends and his country. In an attempt to do something with his life, he enrolled in college, but he had to deal with so much personal guilt, he could not concentrate enough to study. After flunking out his second quarter, he moved to Detroit to work on an automobile assembly line installing bumpers. Mike quit after only five weeks, because the air-powered ratchets sounded too much like machine gun fire, and the sound made him too jumpy. He then hitchhiked around the country, trying to find himself. During this search, he met a lot of people who had experienced varying degrees of personal catastrophes. He found that for many of these people, their catastrophes were merely temporary setbacks. Out of their setbacks, these people arose with renewed strength and greater wisdom than they had before. Mike realized that, even though his life was a psychological mess right now, he might have positive things ahead as well. He began to accept his life as it was: he was a Vietnam veteran and he could do nothing about the past, but he could determine, to a large degree, the life he now lived. Mike began to heal.

A number of veterans reported that they started to get better when they began studying and applying psychology in their lives. The psychologies reported to be of interest to these veterans were Transactional Analysis, Gestalt, Existential, and Psychosynthesis. While the precise therapeutic modality and its validity seemed to be important, perhaps the most consequential aspect was that the veteran began to examine his life authentically.

As I began to examine my life, I found that I did not trust myself, even though the severe degree of my anxiety was lessening. My core fear was that I felt I needed to protect myself from getting lured into another Vietnam experience. I also felt that I had to protect myself from drinking and from wandering into situations where I might be tempted to lose control. To protect myself, I constructed a very potent component to my personality which I termed the "survivor." I view the "survivor" as a domineering, judgmental part of my personality which kept me in total self-control, always striving to do the right thing. To someone who has never experienced making a mess of his life, control is probably no big deal. For me, however, the only thing I desperately needed was the security that came from total control and domination of my impulses. In order to control all impulses, I kept myself at the mercy of the dominating survivor part of me, which was safer than having any choice, since there was the possibility that I might screw it up. Control was assured by my generating scary physical symptoms, such as heart palpitations, intestinal upsets and acute anxiety when I would venture out of the control of the "survivor." These symptoms effectively kept me from venturing into areas where I might react spontaneously and be at the mercy of my impulses, i.e., out of control. I learned to avoid most things fun, because fun meant out of control.

Letting go of this ultra-protective behavior was very difficult for me. It meant I would have to take responsibility for my life, something I just did not have confidence that I could do. How could I trust myself to be responsible for my life when I had screwed it up so badly? I had killed human beings and enjoyed the feelings of power I derived from it. I thought women were of value only as sex objects. I had lied and cheated to get my way. How could I trust myself to take conscious control of my life? This was hard, but I slowly, hesitantly tried. It was a very painful process at first, but as I took more and more risks—as well as the responsibility for their successful outcome—I began to develop increasing levels of self confidence. For example I began to go out with my friends to the bars to dance. I had tremendous impulses to drink, as well as to avoid being responsible for my actions, but I found that I could say no to these impulses and deal with my life. God, it was hard, but I really did it.

One of the greatest insights of my life was realizing that I and I alone had responsibility for my life. While I *knew* I could manage and direct my life, I had trouble *doing* it. Yet, I did do it; I was learning.

I have discussed choice, responsibility and self-control with many other veterans and found we share a common pattern. Prior to examining our lives, we professed to be in charge of our lives, but we clearly were not. We were running our lives on automatic pilot, the automatic pilot of our conditioned responses. This automatic behavior was based on our previous life experiences, in which we drew upon our interactions with our parents, our heroes, and various other significant authority figures in our lives. We thought their influences were our own, but they were the ideals of others with whom we identified. We were living our lives based on the insights of others. For most of us, even when we clearly saw this through psychotherapy, we hesitated to let go and choose for ourselves—authentically. Being aware of and taking full responsibility for one's choices and actions is very, very scary when one is not used to doing it. We were not comfortable taking responsibility for our choices, because if we were wrong, we felt out of control and guilty. We would then lose confidence in our ability to live our lives with self-control.

Many mythological motifs pertaining to the hero's quest actually describe many of the behavior patterns seen in Vietnam veterans. Since these myths are so useful in predicting one's behavior, we can look at them and ask, "Who or what does control our lives?" As previously stated, most veterans live their lives on automatic pilot or in acting out learned behaviors. We feel comfortable with these actions, and when we become consciously aware that much of our lives are lived from these learned behaviors which are now unconscious, we have the option to change what we do not like. When we try to change our ways of living, however, we get extremely tense and anxious because we feel uncomfortable making choices, carrying out those choices, and having to exert our willpower to see them carried out. We are just too used to protecting ourselves from dangers which really do not exist.

I had solved the problem of living my life by turning it over to an idealized, fabricated part of my personality. I built it based on the models provided me by authority figures in my life. This action reduced my tension and anxiety about choice and responsibility because I did not have to consciously deal with any decisions. My internalized authority figure did it for me. But the price I paid for this selling out of myself was a life filled with unhappiness and anxiety. When I recognized what I had done, I began to drop this mask and revert to my authentic self and live my life as I was. It was at this point that I began my "return" journey.

I began to accept myself as I actually was, not as I should be. I recognized that while I was not the toughest person in the world, neither was I the weakest. I was not the smartest person, but I was not the dumbest, either. I began to accept my emotional sensitivity, ultimately even viewing it as a positive attribute. I gave up the idea that I had to be cold and insensitive in order to be a "man." I also accepted that I had intuition, creativity and imagination, which I had considered to be character flaws at one time. I discovered that I could not categorize myself as a particular kind or type of person. I was what I was. While it was difficult to do, I allowed myself, more and more, to be me--the authentic me.

Often in mythological stories, upon finishing the initiation experience, the initiate had two choices concerning his next step. He could refuse the "return," thereby not sharing his discoveries with others, or he could "return," sharing his wisdom and knowledge—his treasure—with others.

Currently many Vietnam veterans are stuck in a "pseudo-return," where they cannot find positive meaning in their experience and hence cannot return with a "treasure" to aid other veterans.

Art, the Marine veteran described in the previous chapter, is one of these persons. He had gone to Vietnam as an infantryman and, of course, experienced much brutal combat. He had also volunteered for many dangerous special missions, to spare married men in his unit from being killed. When Art returned to the United States, he found that he was totally out of synchronization with his society. He was psychologically in Vietnam, but physically in the United States. To reduce his psychic tension over his situation, he began to drink, and drink heavily. By the time he was 27, he was an alcoholic. When he dropped out of American society and went to Mexico to get away from things, he continued to drink and drink and drink. The last time I saw Art, five years ago, he had just returned from Mexico and was being hospitalized for alcoholism at the local Veteran's Administration hospital. He was 36, but looked as though he were 60. His hair was mangy gray and his skin was blue-gray in color; several of his teeth were missing, and his eyes were coated with a yellowish-looking film; he was very skinny and frail, except for the size of his stomach. His stomach was huge. He had somehow developed arthritis in his right leg and needed a cane to help support his walking. His voice was deep and slurry.

As I looked at him, I could only shudder and ask myself where that bright-eyed, adventurous, kind and caring person I once knew had gone. This Art had become a thief and a beggar, caring only from whence and when his next drink was coming. The Art I once knew was dead. That realization was extremely painful for me. Art could not return to society. He was terminally stuck between his past and his present.

Let us now focus briefly on the situation of another Vietnam veteran. Scott, an Army infantryman, also could not "return" to society. After his physical return from Vietnam, he drifted from job to job and from relationship to relationship. He just could not find his niche, his place in life. Finally he left New Jersey and retreated to Wyoming, where he continues to live near the Grand Teton Park. He has retreated from society and chosen not to "return."

However, not all veterans have refused to "return." A minority of combat veterans have made the return passage and integrated themselves back into society. They have something of positive value to offer others in our society. This is the critical point. From an outer perspective, the combat veteran brought nothing of benefit back to society, but after a successful passage of psychotherapy—or sorting out the experience alone—the veteran did bring back an assortment of treasures to share with society. What were some of these treasures?

First, there was self-acceptance. That is, the veteran learned to fully accept himself as he is. He may not approve of what he did or how he did it during the war, but he has accepted his involvement in the war as well as accepted who and what he is.

For me, this was a very difficult task. I felt that accepting my actions was the same as approving them. But as I realized that I did what I thought was necessary at the time and did the best job I could, I found that I could accept my involvement. I acted in the context of the situation in which I found myself. Unfortunately, I was wrong, but once I discovered that I was wrong, I changed my perspective. I could not go back in time and change what I had done in Vietnam, but I could leave the past in the past and go on with my life in the here and now.

Jonathan, a former Marine infantryman, had a similar story. For fifteen years after he returned from combat, he grieved and grieved for his friends who had been killed. During those fifteen years, his life was in limbo. Finally he entered into psychotherapy and ultimately had a revelation leading to the realization that that portion of his life was over. No amount of grieving could ever change the past or bring it back. With this realization, he accepted his present life situation, left the past behind, and went on with his life.

Another category of personal treasure gained by a number of veterans is the ability to be self-directing. Unfortunately, many of the Vietnam veterans are so preoccupied with their pain and suffering that they are not in direct control of their lives. They are instead controlled by feelings and impulses. They are literally like leaves in the wind, blown this way and that at the mercy of the environment.

The combat veteran who has successfully completed the initiation and is in the return phase discovers that he needs to control and direct his life consciously, if he is ever to be happy. When he gave up self-direction, he was running from the mythic, cruel horn of the world. This maneuver was self-defeating; it reinforced his lack of self-direction, and strengthened his avoidance of the world. As

he took control and directed his life in a manner which
was in his best interests, he gained self-confidence and self-
esteem, which promoted his ability to direct himself.

In my case, self-direction came from a strategy my
therapist provided. I call this the Ed Shubat meditation,
named after the clinical psychotherapist who presented it
to me. It goes like this:

Reassure myself that I am a growing, self-actualizing
human being.

Specifically, I am a human being who is a biological
organism, who takes care of himself physically, emotionally,
mentally and spiritually. I deal with situations (physical,
emotional, mental and spiritual) from where I am, as I am,
instead of from a preconceived position.

I learn to deal with myself from a position of what is
best for me, taking into account the background of what
needs to be dealt with. I evaluate my experiences, being
flexible, and act accordingly.

I make attempts at dealing with and processing various
experiences. I take risks and carry out the decisions I make.
I judge and evaluate those decisions, choosing which best
fits me as a person.

I develop self-confidence over time from dealing
authentically with these experiences.

I give positive regard to my humanness, as well as to
the humanness of others, and recognize that I will make
mistakes in my growth process.

For eight years, I meditated on this daily, and was
rewarded by becoming even more self-directed, even more
authentic, and even more autonomous.

Another personal treasure many combat veterans who
returned successfully brought back was a firm sense of
responsibility. No longer could the veteran allow someone
else to think for him. He had to make his own choices
about what he liked, what he wanted to do, how he felt
about something, and where he stood. While it is very
enticing to not take responsibility for one's life, one's
choices, and one's life situation, to a large degree for the
veteran, the consequence of letting someone else do this
for him is the very reason he struggled so after Vietnam.
During the Vietnam war, many of us believed the U.S.
government's political propaganda—at least, at first—that

we were fighting to save the Vietnamese people from communism. Ultimately, though, we found that our government had lied to us. When I first got to Vietnam, I was pro-war. I believed we were there to fight the communists, who were threatening the world. But we were not fighting to save a race of people; we were fighting to protect our own government's blunder. When I discovered that we would take a hill at the expense of six or seven Marines, just to do the same thing over again the next month, I realized that something was wrong. I realized that we were not fighting the war to win it.

Also, another area where we Vietnam veterans were duped was in killing the enemy. Ultimately, most of us killed the NVA, or "gooks," as if they mattered no more than rats. We had successfully been able to dehumanize the entire Vietnamese race. Yet, when we expressed our guilt, many people back home tried to justify our actions by having us rationalize that we had to do it—kill them or they would kill us.

Maybe so, but how many of us veterans ever considered what we were doing? We were just following orders. Many times I have thought to myself, this is how the Germans could have gassed millions of Jews during World War II. They, too, were following orders. This is a point to really consider. I suggest that the reader consider this question: "How far would I go, following orders?"

Those veterans who have successfully returned have had to deal with their involvement in Vietnam and take responsibility for their actions both then and now. To be aware of how one affects other human beings and not knowingly take advantage of them is a sign of being responsible for one's life. This includes lying to women just to get "a piece of ass," cheating on one's wife, or acting in ways which are self-defeating. This is one of the gems the combat veteran—the combat veteran who has successfully returned—can share.

Please note that taking responsibility for our actions is not the same thing as self blame. Naturally, the veteran tended to blame himself for screwing up his life based on his actions in Vietnam. His motto often became, "Vietnam did this to me." As he began to acknowledge that he must take responsibility for his problems stemming from Vietnam, he found that since he got himself into this situation, he had the power to get himself out of it. This realization gave him a tremendous sense of self-empowerment.

Another treasure gained by a number of Vietnam veterans was the realization that they were a valuable part of a web or network of interpersonal relationships. A common occurrence with most "returned" veterans was the tremendously valuable feeling of genuine care and concern of others about their well-being. Many veterans recall that when they were in the most unbearable pain and when they had been rejected by almost everyone they knew, there were usually to be found one or two people who stood behind them through thick and thin. Interestingly, it was not until the veterans were on the road to psychological recovery that they were able to acknowledge openly that if it had not been for those persons who really cared, they never would have made it.

In my own case, after I returned form Vietnam, I was rejected by everyone I knew. I was sure my friends could sense the pain I was in, especially since I had to stay drunk. I still remember that one of my close friends confided in me—at the lowest period in my life—while we sat in a bar drinking, that I was really "fucked up" and not fun to be with anymore. I knew this, but I did not know what to do about it or where to go for help to solve my dilemma. Had he stabbed me with a knife, the pain would have been less. It was not long, though, before my wife became overwhelmed with my problems, as did my friends. No one felt comfortable with me, since they could not relate to me, and ultimately very few people wanted to be with me. However, one person did stand behind me. He was the third psychotherapist I saw. Even today, I shudder to think what would have become of me had Ed Shubat not taken more than just a "professional interest" in me. I am sure I either would have killed myself or had to be institutionalized. That psychotherapist—whom I did not even like at first—was my total, psychological support system. He was behind me when I quit drinking, when I went back to college and needed help from the VA to finance the endeavor, and when I went to graduate school; he was my best man in my second marriage. Finally, even when he was within days of dying from cancer, he still was there for me. Just before he died I asked him to find me when I die, if there is an afterlife. He assured me that he would. To be truly appreciated for "me," in spite of my life's background, was a real treasure.

Self-reliance was reported by a number of veterans to be a tremendously valuable gained asset. Self-reliance came to these men because they had to face combat "alone"; they had to face death "alone"; they had to return to America and put their lives back in order "alone." Since they were used to being alone, they did not require the constant support and reassurance that so many of their noncombatant peers needed when making life transitions or adjusting to situations beyond their control. For example, these veterans did not get in a major turmoil about what the recession would do to them. Most reasoned that if they survived Vietnam, they could survive any economic downturn; those who worked in the corporate world believed they could survive the corporate wheeling and dealing. Some reported that they did not become emotionally immobilized when their wives left them. If they could survive Vietnam, they could survive a divorce. There just was not anything life could deal to this person that could be worse than what he experienced in Vietnam.

From a larger perspective, he brought back with him the knowledge that going to a war may be necessary at times, but attacking a country would require more justification than its political orientation. The financial, psychological and human costs were far too great. Imagine being the parents of an 18- or 19-year-old male. Much of your life's energy has been diverted and channeled into aiding him during his growth process, from teaching him to dress himself as a pre-schooler to teaching him to drive a car as a teen-ager. How would you respond when you were told your son had just been killed in a war that served no purpose? Imagine how the parents of a Vietnam soldier killed in action must feel. Imagine how they must agonize that his dying was for nothing. While there are times when we need to stand up—even to fight to our death—for something, the cause must be truly worthwhile. No human life is worth wasting for another Vietnam-type of situation— no human life.

Finally, another piece of treasure several veterans

reported was their feeling that they were part of a larger system of life emanating through the universe. That is, they felt a spiritual sense of being "at one" with the universe. This was an authentic experience for these veterans, not a religious belief. They could not explain it, but they were cognizant of it.

Perhaps this transcendent attitude was elicited by their inner search for meaning in their lives. As the veterans were forced to truly look inside themselves for answers to life, they found them at the core of their being. That core, which may be considered to be their life essence, is what they feel connects them to the rest of the universe.

For me, the discovery of my essence was quite an event. I had read for years about people who were in touch with what they described as their higher selves, their souls, or the atman; but to me, those were but plays of words. Then one day I imagined I was walking up a mountain; at the top of that mountain, I met a wise old man. I asked him what was going on with me, and he told me. I knew this was the key to connection with my deeper, authentic self. The wise old man was an objective symbol of what I consider to be my deeper self, for lack of a better label. I have benefited beyond words by coming into contact with this deeper aspect of myself, which I call "Big D," for Big Daryl. It is a wise, non-judgemental, accepting part of me, and it has served as my anchor point for the last several years. Just by making contact with this part of me, everything I feel about my entire Vietnam experience has been a beneficial lesson. Through losing myself in Vietnam, I have found myself.

In this chapter I have described aspects of the "return" of the veteran from a mythological approach. While some veterans have successfully made the return and benefited from it, most have not. Now it is the job of the returnees to share their "gold and treasure" with those veterans stuck in the "pseudo-return." With this in mind, let me review the grim situation which faces more than eighty percent (80%) of combat veterans today—those stuck in the "pseudo-return."

6
THE SITUATION OF THE STUCK VETERAN

"Sometimes you win, sometimes you lose."
—Carol King

"Every man's condition is a solution."
—Emerson

"Where you are, I was/Where I am, you will be."
—tattoo seen on dead Marine's arm

*A*s we have seen in the previous chapter, those veterans who were able to reintegrate themselves into society were the ones who gained valuable insights from their Vietnam experience and made the successful return. Let us turn our attention to the Vietnam veterans who still have not returned, the ones who are stuck in the pseudo-return.

During the two decades following the Vietnam war, a number of researchers have studied Vietnam veterans to discover if those "stuck" veterans felt they had gleaned any positive benefits from their service in Vietnam. For the majority, the answer to those studies has been no—no from: 1) the psychological effects of killing other humans, 2) being in danger of being killed by other humans, 3) the disregard for any value of life, 4) the environment, and 5) the lack of purpose for their involvement in the war. Most veterans are casualties of a senseless war in which they were betrayed by their government and its citizens. Unlike the middle eastern war (specifically, Desert Storm), the military in Vietnam was not allowed to fight the war to win it. There was no homecoming celebration; there was only guilt, remorse and despair. This has contributed to the large number of personal psychological disasters experienced by Vietnam veterans.

For example, alcohol and drug abuse are reportedly five times greater among Vietnam veterans than in their peers. The divorce rate is four times greater, the suicide rate is 2.5 times greater, and unemployment is three times greater than non-combat peers. Our country has assumed the responsibility of helping these veterans facilitate the healing of their physical and psychological wounds. However, psychological healing is largely dependent on professional counselors and therapists with an adequate understanding of the phenomonological effects of war. That is, the psychological health care professionals must understand the emotional, mental and spiritual ravages of war. They must attempt to comprehend the guilt, despair and abandonment that haunts the Vietnam veteran.

To treat a veteran as an object to be "fixed" through a series of psychological techniques is doomed to failure. The helping professional must step into the shoes of the veteran and view his current life in the context of the veteran's Vietnam experiences, the social conflict experienced by the veteran, and our society's insistence on ignoring the veteran because of the war's negative outcome. Unfortunately, most Vietnam veterans have been unable to overcome the trauma of the experience, a deficiency which has tended to alienate the Vietnam veteran from society even further.

The shadow of the Vietnam war continues to stress the lives of Vietnam veterans in six basic categories:

1) difficulties in readjusting to civilian life,
2) differences between Vietnam veterans and veterans of other wars,
3) relationship of the Vietnam veteran's pre-combat dispositional factors to his adjustment problems after the war,
4) the combat ordeal producing post-war adjustment problems,

5) current psychological strategies for treating disturbed Vietnam veterans, and

6) the social and political alienation of Vietnam veterans.

Most Vietnam combat veterans faced problems readjusting to civilian life, the first category mentioned. Many veterans, upon their return to the United States, felt as though they were aliens on a strange planet. They were misfits, no longer in the military and no longer able to fit in with their friends or to function in society. Even today, many veterans are no more integrated into civilian life than they were twenty-five years ago. Many have a string of unsuccessful relationships; many cannot get or hold meaningful jobs, and others drift from city to city, year after year, trying to "straighten out their heads." Quite a few have tried to numb the pain of their situation by excessive use of alcohol and/or drugs. In the final analysis, they are stuck in a hellish limbo. They are filled with emotional pain and suffering accompanied by feelings of anguish, total despair, rejection, self-hate, and an almost unbearable guilt for their involvement in Vietnam.

Art, the former Marine infantryman who is now a "street person," gave up twelve-and-a-half years ago. Life lost its meaning for him, not as a result of specific combat incidents, but out of his general, existential loneliness. Life had become a cruel joke whose only purpose was to have fun: sex, sun and suds. How could life have meaning? It was a struggle to survive, and ultimately, you died anyway. Life was absurd. He tried to make sense of his life and where he fit into it, but he could not. Each day, he tried to find a reason to justify his life, and each day he failed. He found that alcohol could take the cruel edge off of life, so he drank more and more. Presently, he drinks one quart of vodka a day. When I talked with him while writing this book, he told me that he would pay me $100.00 to shoot him in the head when he did not expect it. He did not want to know when death would come to him, but he pleaded that it come soon, very soon. He mumbled something about the agony he was in, then he fell into a drunken sleep. That was many months ago, and I have not seen him since. While this is but one example, there are thousands of stuck Vietnam veterans still existing in that type of pure hell.

The second category of stress the Vietnam veteran experiences is based in the fundamental difference between him and veterans of other wars. Vietnam veterans did not win the war and have been reminded of this repeatedly by both World War II and Korean veterans. The shame Vietnam veterans experience over this loss has caused them to repress many aspects of the war; this has prevented them from being able to work through it psychologically.

Pete, an Army infantry officer, summed this up well. Pete's father was a highly decorated B-17 bomber pilot during World War II. Two of his brothers were killed in action, one in Iwo Jima and the other in France. Pete had to follow in those footsteps in Vietnam. When he came back, however, he just could not face his father. Pete felt as though he had let both his father and his country down by losing the war. When Pete and his father went to the local VFW post for a couple of drinks, not a word was spoken about Vietnam. Yet Pete could see the frustration in his father's eyes. Pete thought all his efforts had been for naught. As Pete put it, "How could I face anyone? I participated in a war we lost."

How could the United States have won the Vietnam war? The military's hands were tied. Many United States politicians expected to intimidate the North Vietnamese into submission. In reality, we had to fight a tough, determined, and resistant opponent--the North Vietnamese soldier. We as a country just could not make a commitment to fight a war with little purpose. We had a very powerful military, but we had no solid political and social support to back it. For political reasons, we could not just leave the country. So we, as infantrymen, were essentially offered as a sacrifice, to buy a just retreat. This situation was not satisfactory to previous veterans. They could not understand how Vietnam was different from World War II.

The third category concerns problematic factors common to veterans which significantly contribute to stress and adjustment. While not all Vietnam veterans were psychologically predisposed to adjustment difficulties, a number of those who are "stuck," who failed to make the return, are. Many military volunteers were "running" from themselves by joining the military. They felt that going to Vietnam would somehow "straighten" them out. A very common perception among the Marine Corps volunteers was that the Marine Corps could take you, an inadequate "boy," and make you a "man." In fact, the recruitment slogan used by the Marine Corps was, "The Marine Corps builds men." Since these men already felt inadequate and lacked self-confidence and self-direction, they were predisposed to psychological adjustment disorders. The burdens of the war were harder for them to bear; the social approval they had strived for turned out to be social rejection.

Roger, an Army helicopter gunner, stated that he joined the Army because it would make him a man. People would respect him then. He worked hard in boot camp, doing well in marksmanship, physical endurance, and combat skills. In Vietnam, he worked hard at his mission—killing Vietnamese. Yet, upon his return to the United States, he found that instead of more respect from his peers, he now had less. Deeply troubled, he ultimately went into psychotherapy, only to discover that his problems were not solely Vietnam-caused. He found that he felt inadequate as a person many years before going into the military. For Roger, the military service was a way for him to compensate for being "weak"—an objective like that of Teddy Roosevelt, who joined the "Rough Riders" to compensate for his poor health and poor eyesight.

I think most of us who volunteered for the military share Roger's situation. We, too, felt a sense of inadequacy in ourselves. We needed a boost to our egos that we felt the military would provide. However, the military did not compensate for our feelings of inadequacy. When one needs to prove to himself that he is brave, strong and adequate, he will often put himself through a series of self-imposed tests and trials. No matter the outcome, adequacy is never proven. Proof comes only through learning to accept oneself for what he is.

The fourth category of adjustment problems is based on the actual, traumatic combat experiences of the veterans. These experiences caused post-war adjustment problems, to some degree, to nearly every combat veteran who served in Vietnam. True, many of the World War II veterans had this social readjustment problem when they returned home from the war, but not nearly to the degree we find it in the Vietnam veteran. The World War II veteran's mission was clear; he also had tremendous support from his country. The Vietnam veteran had neither of these. More than likely, he was belittled and made to feel like a criminal. He was alienated from a society that sent him to fight in a war supported only half-heartedly. The noncommitted position of the United States has hurt more Vietnam veterans than all the physical and emotional wounds received in combat— at least tenfold. This, in my opinion, was the ultimate betrayal of the veteran by his country.

Tom was an Army officer with the 101st Airborne Division in Vietnam. After being involved in college ROTC for four years and graduating in 1969, he was commissioned and sent to Vietnam. He felt pride in the military and chose to perform the best that he could in combat. Tom was wounded by a mortar round which severed his spinal cord, and he was paralyzed from the waist down. After he was discharged from the service, he found that he could not get a job in his field, finance, mainly due to his disability. He was told confidentially that customers coming into a bank for a loan did not want to deal with disabled people, especially one who was a Vietnam veteran. Tom was devastated. He had gone to Vietnam with the perception of protecting his society. Now he was permanently disabled--a consequence of his fighting for a society that now turned its back on him because his disability might remind them of the war. Tom gave up twenty years ago, lives solely on a government disability pension, and passes his days drinking.

While most Americans would argue that it was the *government* who sent Tom to Vietnam, not them, my questions is this: "Who voted in the politicians of the time?" It is the citizens who make up our society. Society did not want then, and does not want now, to deal with the casualties of Vietnam.

The fifth category, that of the treatment strategies used for disturbed Vietnam veterans, has been a tremendous problem for the "stuck" veteran. The major reasons for this problem are: a) the wrong method of psychotherapeutic treatment and b) inadequate training of the counselor or therapist for the needs of the combat veteran.

The first is often the most problematic for the veteran. In training, whether for psychiatry, for clinical psychology, or for marriage and family counseling, the health care professional's philosophy of treatment is based on the psychological orientation of the training school. For example, psychiatrists must complete a four-year medical school program which is followed by a two-year psychiatric program. The main treatment modality is pharmacological, which stems from a medical background grounded in biochemistry. Hence, symptoms of depression or anxiety in patients tend to be viewed as a biochemical imbalance. Because of this view, psychiatrists traditionally spend very little time actually talking with the patient as a way of working through their problems.

Clinical psychologists have considerably more training in psychology than do psychiatrists and tend to view many psychological disorders as learned, maladaptive behavior. Since the majority of universities have tried to make psychology a legitimate "science," they tend to train and teach a behavior-oriented psychotherapy, which is rooted in learning models.

Counselors, on the other hand, can be trained in social welfare, in psychology, or in career counseling. Generally, they do not attempt to "change" overt behavior or perform psychotherapy. Rather, they tend to take a more passive stance, allowing the client to become more in touch with his problems and work through them in his own way.

While each of these three modes is useful when working with veterans, a problem arises in selecting the appropriate form of treatment. Unfortunately, too often each practitioner sees his or her way as *the* way. That is, the psychiatrist tends to view the combat veteran's problems exclusively as biochemical imbalances. Any phenomena that do not fit in the model taught to the psychiatrist are simply ignored or pathologized.

The clinical psychologist, if behavior-oriented, tends to view the combat veteran's problems exclusively as maladaptive learning. That is, the veteran has learned to live successfully in a war situation which is no longer present. Therefore, the veteran needs to extinguish his former conditioning and learn appropriate social behavior, which will allow him to adjust to civilian life. Any phenomena that do not fit into this model are, again, ignored or explained solely from a behavior model.

The counselor tends to view the combat veteran's problems as not being in touch with himself. Hence, he or she poses reflective questions, such as, "I can feel you are in pain. What is the pain like for you?" The combat veteran will then tell of the excruciating pain he is in. The counselor will then reflect the veteran's response, perhaps repeating his exact words. Unfortunately, often the veteran becomes more aware of the pain with this technique, but has no "tools" to facilitate his growth.

I want to emphasize that each of these three modes of treatment can be beneficial when used appropriately. But when the health care professional tries to place the veteran into his or her own model of reality, the veteran is further alienated. The health care professional can speak of problems theoretically and academically for the rest of the veteran's life and still never successfully contribute to the veteran's well-being. The effective health care professional must learn what existence is like for the veteran today; that is, he or she must learn about the veteran's existential position. What is it like to be that veteran physically, emotionally, and spiritually? These questions should be answered before the therapist chooses a mode of treatment. The therapeutic session must be between two individuals as they are: human beings.

By learning to see reality from the veteran's perspective, the health care professional can truly begin to help the veteran. It is critical to remember that each combat veteran is a unique individual with unique life experiences, and he must be treated as a unique person with unique problems. Otherwise, the therapist will never form a therapeutic bridge to work with the veteran. Once an authentic connection with the combat veteran's unique, existential problems has begun, specific treatment modalities can be used as they are appropriate. While each health care professional has his or her own psychological approach, he or she must bridge that approach to ameliorate the patient's existential situation. Each patient requires a unique, psychotherapeutic strategy based on his needs, not the therapist's.

The sixth category of readjustment disorder stems from the general, political alienation of the veteran. By alienation, I mean to say that the veteran feels rejected and unsupported by the society he sought to support, denounced by both social and political systems in the United States. While this atmosphere was not meant to alienate Vietnam veterans, it did. Veterans went to Vietnam with at least the pseudo support of their society, but they returned to ridicule and condemnation.

These six categories are the basis of the "limbo" state in which many Vietnam veterans find themselves. I seriously doubt if one can categorize a veteran's dilemma into just one of the specific categories. Rather, I think most post-war problems are combinations and permutations of all six categories, varying with the individual and his life situation.

Having considered the "stuck" Vietnam veteran, what is the next point to contemplate? Can those veterans who have made a successful "return" teach anything of value to those who are "stuck"? How can this be done?

7
FINDING THE GOLD

"The path you are on is the one which was made for you."
—old saying

*"Open your eyes and see
it is you, yourself, you have searched for all these years.*
—E.E. Shubat, psychotherapist

*"The way which can be told is not the way.
It must be found through your own vision."*
—Interpretation of Tao Te Ching

*P*revious chapters contain in some detail what the veterans who made the "return" have brought back with them, in terms of positive meaning from their experiences. This chapter consists of suggestions from those veterans who made it, to those who are stuck in the labyrinth or maze, about what is needed to get out of the maze.

The first point is dealing with guilt. So many veterans feel that they were not strong because they were afraid during combat, did not see as much combat as they felt was necessary to justify wrecking their lives, or that they enjoyed the killing too much. This is the tyranny of the way *things should be*. The *shoulds* are what kill the life direction of so many veterans. What should or should not have happened needs to be replaced with "what is." If the stuck veteran cannot walk down a street alone, all the *shoulds* in the world will not change this situation. This is the current situation of the veteran. It has no ultimate value as being good or bad. The veteran does not have to like it, but he needs to own it. To run from and deny the situation does no good. To finally be honest with oneself—that one is in a living hell—is necessary. It holds no relationship with being weak or inadequate. It just is.

In my own case, when I got back from Vietnam, I tried to keep the pain and rage inside by drinking. I felt that, since I was a Marine, I *should* not have any pain. I forgot that I was a human being beneath the "Marine cloak" and could not destroy my fundamental nature. Being human, with feelings, I was allowed to hurt without having to justify my pain. This was hard because my combat veteran friends, as well as my family, advised me to "not think about it," "be strong," or "not let it bother me." Yet I thought about my pain every minute of my waking day. I tried to be strong, but I felt so vulnerably weak; and it *did* bother me. Their advice was offered in love and out of their own despair over my condition, but it did not work. I became increasingly alienated from myself. I split myself into essentially two beings—what I should be versus what I felt I was. It was not until I hit the bottom and felt like taking my life that I admitted to myself the agony in which I was living.

This brings me to the second point. Once the veteran admits that he is in an agonizing situation, it is time to get psychotherapeutic help. There are many therapists, but only a few who will have the necessary "therapeutic fit" for him, in order for him to get well. Rarely will the first therapist the veteran sees have the proper "therapeutic fit."

Therapeutic fit refers to a mutual relationship in which there exists mutual caring, positive regard for each other, mutual respect, and basic trust.

Kevin, an Army mortar man, described the process as follows: When I started having anxiety attacks, I was referred to a psychiatrist by the emergency room physician. I told the psychiatrist that I was in deep conflict over the Vietnam thing. He was not so concerned with that, but concentrated on my symptoms. He gave me a prescription for tranquilizers, anti-depressants and sleeping pills.

Everything was pretty good for a week or two, but I could tell the valium was not working so well any more.

So the psychiatrist upped the dosage. Each time he increased the dosage, I would be alright for another couple of weeks, but then I would start to feel anxious again. I found that I could take away some of the edge of the anxiety by taking a couple of drinks of whiskey. This cycle went on for one whole year. I was heavily dependent on tranquilizers and alcohol, and I re-focused from Vietnam to just keeping my tension down.

Finally, I went to another psychiatrist in a large city, to see if he could help me more. The same cycle was re-instituted. Then I joined a transactional analysis group. The men and women in the group, I could feel, cared more about me. I was not just a "thing." The leader of the group asked me many questions about how I felt. I could not believe it! Things were so different. I quit the group because it moved too fast for me, but I did check out a clinical psychologist and, for some reason, I stayed with him for a few sessions. I did not like the guy at first, but after a couple of sessions, I began to trust him. He did not push me faster than I wanted to go, yet he would not let me continue with my bullshit without confronting me. We worked through the Vietnam thing together and even parts of my early childhood, which had kicked off much of my trouble. My advice to others is to stay in the consumer mode. Do not trust a therapist about whom you just have a bad feeling. About three months is the limit I would see someone without seeing some positive results. Then go to someone else until you find one that can help you.

The veteran will know when he has met a therapist with whom he can have that therapeutic fit. The process is very similar to getting to know people. With some people, one can spend only a little time, revealing very little, contriving to avoid being corrected or belittled. With others, one can reveal all and still feel accepted, still maintaining the presence of one who has his own personality. The second state is the state the Vietnam veteran is wise to search for. Until it is found, very little can be gained therapeutically.

The third bit of advice to the combat client/patient is to not expect to feel better at first. As the veteran describes and relives the situational cause of this pain, much conflict will arise. This pain is not just one more useless, needless agonizing pain. This pain is that of working through the impasses in one's life. It is an agonizing, yet necessary, process in psychotherapy.

When I first started to reveal to my therapist what I had done in Vietnam and how guilty I felt, I thought for sure that he, too, would abandon me. I could visually see him clutching his throat and gasping in horror as he fell from his chair over the disgusting, disgraceful things I had done in Vietnam. When I did tell him and felt he would kick me out of his office, he merely said, "Thank God that is out in the open now." He did not reject me.

Over the next several months, however, I felt the agonizing torture and pain of having to relive some of my experiences. It was pure hell—pure hell during the sessions and pure hell after the sessions. It was pure hell second after second, minute after minute, hour after hour, day after day, until I had worked through it. Then most of the pain vanished, just like that.

The veteran's knowing what he has to go through does not make it easier. Try to prepare for the pain of holding your finger directly over a burning candle. One cannot. One must experience it in its fullness.

The fourth point still applies: one can better live out the ordeal by having a support system. The combat veteran needs to recognize that during the course of therapy, he will experience much tension and anxiety. There will be times when he will feel off base, not know where to turn, and be confused about himself. This is a normal process but can feel like pure hell. This is the time when a support system is critical. The support system offers the veteran positive regard and support for who he is and what he is experiencing. This offers the veteran firm ground to support his efforts to find himself. He can then experience what is necessary for his particular therapeutic situation without fear of rejection. This has an incredibly stabilizing effect on the veteran.

John, an Army infantry officer, describes his experience this way:

> When I came back from Vietnam, everything was different. I did not know who I was, what I was or where I should be going in my life. I was off balance. But since I was perceived as a tough combat veteran, I felt that if I told anyone how off

balance I felt, I would somehow be a very weak person. So, at first, I played the role of a tough infantry officer. But I became more and more cynical, more unhappy and more confused. I wanted to drop the whole stage performance and tell everyone, including myself, how scared and miserable I was. But where could I go? There was no psychological support systems that I knew of at the time. So I found another answer, that of drinking. I began to live my life with a little on-going "buzz." It blunted the sharp sting of life's cruel horror. But soon, I found myself drinking more and more. Within two years, I was a drunk. I was hospitalized in an alcohol treatment program and during that time, something marvelous occurred. Several representatives from Alcoholics Anonymous (A.A.) visited me. I decided to join A.A. and to my surprise, I found a very supportive group of people who had been "there." They had hit the bottom in their lives and now were working their way back. They gave me the strength to deal with Vietnam just by being accepting. I could question my motives, my life, anything, and they did not judge me. After I had this support base, I used it to launch my life. I quit drinking. I learned a lot about the benefits of a support group from that experience.

The fifth point is for the veteran to be patient and nurturant with himself and his therapeutic task. Recovering from an emotional disorder is a bumpy road. One day it will seem as though the conflict is gone, but the next day, the conflict is worse. This up and down process, though frustrating and painful, is the way the therapeutic process works. This turmoil and suffering are for gain, but it is not an ordeal of *useless* suffering.

I can remember my own experience of the road. As I mention in an earlier chapter, I would go out on picnics and outings, but find myself very uneasy. I would imagine that the NVA were behind the pine trees, stalking me. I would imagine that lightning storms were incoming rocket and mortar attacks and that exploding firecrackers were rifle shots aimed at me. I felt this way even when I was in my biofeedback desensitization program and knew that the enemy were not stalking me, lightning was not a rocket attack, and firecrackers' "bangs" were not gunfire. I still strongly felt as though I was under attack. This was very confusing for me. One part knew nothing was wrong, but the other screamed, "Under attack!" I would have periods when I could enjoy life without the fear of being killed, but they were always followed by a panic or anxiety period when I was not sure whether I was really in danger. Finally, as I let the panic attacks just happen and began to nurture and support myself, they began to die down and almost completely diminish.

The sixth and final point is to acknowledge and accept that giving up the pain of Vietnam is not easy. The combat veteran has lived his pain for so long that it has become an integral part of him. As he gets better, though, he will have to give it up. This is hard, however, for as terrible as the pain is, it is familiar. Thus the transition is often anxiety-producing. It can feel as if one is becoming complacent. As one learns to give up the pain and accept that he really can have a productive and happy life, the resistance to healing will subside.

Often, people who have not been emotionally wounded wonder why it is so difficult to give up the pain and suffering of a traumatic disorder. Since the veteran has experienced so much pain in his life, he has grown accustomed to it and often thinks that life is pain. He cannot relate to people or a lifestyle of self-fulfillment and self-actualization because his world is one of total danger. Most of his day is concerned with maneuvers to protect himself from dangers and destruction. Since his constructed reality is one in which the world is a very dangerous place, if he is to survive, he must constantly be vigilant and guarded. He also feels that no one can like or appreciate him for who he is. Instead he feels that there must be an angle or ulterior reasons for others' wanting to be with him. While his constructed reality is distorted, it is his reality.

As the veteran gradually learns to give up his defenses and protection from the world, he feels very vulnerable. As he feels vulnerable, he tends to re-erect his defensive posture to the world. Gradually, as time goes on, he lets go of his protective devices more and more until he, at last, sides with health and begins to respect his true wants, desires, wishes, and aspirations, instead of protecting himself from the world.

These changes, however, are usually a very slow process and need to be respected as such. As the veteran learns to take small risks over time, he builds his self-confidence and can then feel more comfortable with ever more assertiveness.

AFTERWORD

*I*t has been more than twenty-five years since I served in Vietnam, but many of the images are as fresh as today's. As I look back over the difficult path I and others have traveled to heal from the Vietnam experience, I am very grateful.

I am grateful that I found the support I needed to make the "return" positive, but there was more to it than that. Giving up the ghost of Vietnam required a tremendous amount of my energy. For me and other veterans, putting the Vietnam experience in perspective gave us strength-- strength not only to overcome the psychic damage from the Vietnam experience, but also to transcend it and to find meaning, a true blessing.

In the fall of 1992, having worked for the same medical product testing company for ten years, I was terminated. I had brought to fruition many new medical product developments and testing procedures, but I did not fit in.

I did the unimaginable. I began my own medical testing company on my desk at home, with only $3,297 to my name. I had no real entrepreneurial experience and no co-workers for support. I had only myself, my education, and the ability to keep on going in spite of the anxiety and terror of failing.

I learned from my experiences in Vietnam that if I was to get what I wanted, I would have to pay the price and work for it. There was no silver spoon available. I learned from Vietnam how to face obstacles—alone. In Vietnam,

67

as I have previously stated, I had to face my combat fears—alone—as well as deal with the fear of being killed—alone. Like other Vietnam veterans, I had to deal with my life back in the United States—alone.

I believe I could not have started my company, BioScience Laboratories, Inc., with virtually no money, no support, and no co-workers, had I not endured the pain and agony of Vietnam. Now, after two years, BioScience has become a debt-free corporation consisting of three laboratories employing eighteen scientists.

I have witnessed similar drive and stamina in other Vietnam veterans who have returned. I say to my fellow veterans: *Never doubt the power of your Vietnam experience to serve as a catalyst to launch you to greater things.*

I ask you, my brother veterans, to use your experience of war to make your lives better and more meaningful. You are the best this country has produced. You need only to see it, believe it, and—most of all—honor it, for *you are the hero who has found the grail. It is you.*

RECOMMENDED READING

Assaqioli, R. *Psychosynthesis*. Viking, 1972.

Colodzin, B. *How To Survive Trauma*. Laramie, Wyoming: Station Hill Press, 1993.

Daniels, V and Horowitz, L.J. *Being And Caring: A Psychology For Living*, 2nd Ed. Mayfield Publishing, 1984.

Feinstein, D. and S. Krippner. *Personal Mythology*. Los Angeles: Jeremy P. Tarcher, 1988.

Kornfield, J. *A Path With Heart*. Tarcher Publishing, 1993.

Frankl, V.E. *Man's Search For Meaning*. Beason Press, 1992

Lifton, R.J. *Home From The War: Vietnam Veterans, Neither Victims Nor Executioner*. New York: Touchstone Books, 1973.

Hellman, J. *American Myth and The Legacy Of Vietnam*. New York: Columbia University Press, 1986.

Maslow, A.H. *The Farther Reaches of Human Nature*. Viking, 1972

Sullivan, L.E. *Icanchu's Drum: An Orientation To Meaning In South American Religions*. New York: Macmillan, 1988.

ABOUT THE AUTHOR

Daryl S. Paulson, Ph. D. is the President and CEO of BioScience Laboratories, Inc., a medical/pharmaceutical product research firm. He has doctorates in both psychology and Human Science with emphasis in psychoneuroimmunolgy. Dr. Paulson served in the U.S. Marine Corps with Infantry units of the 1st Marine Division. He was awarded the Navy Commendation Medal with the Combat V for Valor, the Vietnamese Cross of Gallantry, and the Combat Action Award.

Additional copies of
WALKING THE POINT
by Daryl S. Paulson, PhD.,
may be ordered by sending a check or
money order for $11.95 postpaid for
each copy to:

Daryl S. Paulson, Ph.D.
316 North 20th Avenue
Bozeman, MT 59718

Quantity discounts are also available
from the publisher.